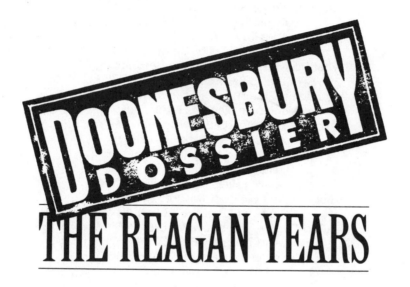

DOONESBURY DOSSIER

THE REAGAN YEARS

·G. B. TRUDEAU·
DOONESBURY DOSSIER

THE REAGAN YEARS

INTRODUCTION BY GLORIA STEINEM

HOLT, RINEHART AND WINSTON
NEW YORK

Copyright © 1980, 1981, 1982, 1983, 1984 by G.B. Trudeau
Introduction copyright © 1984 by Holt, Rinehart and Winston
All rights reserved, including the right to reproduce
this book or portions thereof in any form.
Published by Holt, Rinehart and Winston,
383 Madison Avenue, New York, New York 10017.
Published simultaneously in Canada by Holt, Rinehart
and Winston of Canada, Limited.

Library of Congress Catalog Card Number: 84-80587
ISBN Hardbound: 0-03-061729-4
ISBN Paperback: 0-03-000072-6

First Edition

Designer: Paul Gamarello/Eyetooth Design
Printed in the United States of America

The cartoons in this book have appeared in newspapers
in the United States and abroad under the auspices of
Universal Press Syndicate.

10 9 8 7 6 5 4 3 2 1

ISBN 0-03-061729-4 HARDBOUND
ISBN 0-03-000072-6 PAPERBACK

For Biff and Rickie

INTRODUCTION BY
GLORIA STEINEM

·Four Good Reasons for Reading This Book·
(ANY ONE OF WHICH SHOULD BE ENOUGH)

By way of research for writing this, I read the introductions—written by Garry Wills and William F. Buckley, Jr., respectively—for the first and second big *Doonesbury* anthologies.

The Wills essay was a well-researched report on the early characters and characteristics of *Doonesbury*'s world. Its premise was that this new-style comic strip's success and trademark came from carrying a hip sportscasting style into social comment on every area of American life. "Almost every one of us so-called adult male Americans," Wills explained in his very first sentence, "is a jock manqué."

The Buckley essay was a personal account of his surprise at liking something as frivolous as a comic strip. Buckley explained that he first heard of Garry Trudeau while looking at "the names of people fetching honorary degrees" at Yale, and finally read a collection of *Doonesbury* strips only after being asked to write an introduction. "There are the anticlimaxes," Buckley notes in his role of critic, "but the reader forgives them indulgently; he is well enough nourished, all the more so since there is all that wonderful assonant humor and derision in mid-panel; indeed, not infrequently the true climaxes come in the penultimate panel, and the rest is lagniappe."

Well, I am neither a jock manqué nor a Yale man. I am not crazy about phrases like "not infrequently," people who say "fetching" (unless they are British), and commentary phrased like Buckley's "the longueurs are sometimes almost teasingly didactic." Therefore you might wonder why three such disparate people should be writing praisefully about one and the same creation.

This proves the first virtue of Trudeau's work: it brings very diverse people together. Because *Doonesbury*'s world stretches from campus to Washington, from American bedrooms and football fields to the battlefields of the Mideast and American blunders in Southeast Asia, it includes more varieties of characters than any other comic strip, not to mention more than most movies or novels. No wonder the readers who find themselves connected by their mutual liking for *Doonesbury* are very diverse indeed. What else could be shared by arch-conservative William Buckley, who does not even think female Americans should be included equally in the Constitution, as well as by me and other feminists; or, for that matter, by Garry Trudeau himself, who also campaigned long and hard for the Equal Rights Amendment and for feminist politicians? Not much.

Such bringing together could not be accomplished by papering over or downplaying real differences of opinion, and Trudeau would never attempt that. On the contrary, he uses the differences themselves as the source of much of the humor in *Doonesbury*. Furthermore, no character, whatever her or his beliefs, gets past the Trudeau pen without the little inconsistencies that make us human and vulnerable and that allow even our deepest enemies to become mysteriously understandable. Right smack in the middle of a real conflict, passionate belief, or confrontation, there arrives that moment of uncertainty or endearing personal *schreck*—often in, as Buckley would say, "the penultimate panel"—that allows us to smile and empathize with each other.

The second reason to read this book has to do with change. If this doesn't sound too pushy, it even has to do with redemption.

Unlike most of his comic colleagues who refuse to let their characters age, much less change their minds or personal styles, Trudeau's people grow, take on new ideas, change their jobs and even their personal worlds. For instance: Joanie Caucus, a burgeoning feminist, managed to live more or less peacefully in a campus commune with a jock who chose only the most obedient of girlfriends, young women whom Joanie tried valiantly to subvert. The jock took his turn at communal cooking, even if he did so with his football helmet on. When he had to go off to Vietnam, we realized just how vulnerable, and how valuable, a mindless jock could be. The same Joanie became campaign manager for Ginny Slade, a black woman with the courage to run for Congress, and with a boyfriend named Clyde who didn't think she should be a candidate at all; yet Clyde campaigns for her in white racist neighborhoods and finally admits that he is proud of her. Lacey Davenport, a patrician Congresswoman fairly distant from brand-new-lawyer Joanie's homemaker background and liberal/radical beliefs, nonetheless hires her as a Congressional aide out of respect for Joanie's past behavior in the opposition camp. Rick Redfern, an egocentric Washington investigative reporter, falls in love with Joanie and (almost) allows her to save him from becoming a gossip columnist for *People* magazine. The list of changes and surprising personal journeys goes on and on. Even the worst terrorist, the most pure of female Maoists, the most vacuous of television commentators, or the least competent of Presidents may turn out to have a saving grace and a change of heart.

This gives us faith. If the *Doonesbury* characters we love and identify with can change and be redeemed, surely we, the readers, can change and be redeemed too.

Of course, none of this would be possible if Trudeau did not *like* his characters; or, to say the same thing in a more realistic way, if he were not capable of seeing at least one touching quality in people he doesn't like very much, and at least one inconsistency in people he likes and admires.

This talent for empathy, the third reason for reading this book, also separates Trudeau from the Jules Feiffer–ish tradition that, given the political content they both share, would otherwise be an obvious parallel. Feiffer's world yields a kind of amusement and instruction that is similar to *Doonesbury,* but his people make us feel a little superior; a dead giveaway of the fact that their creator probably feels a little superior to them, too.

According to H.W. Fowler's classic definitions of the purposes of various forms of humorous comment, this means that Feiffer's function is more that of satire and sarcasm, whose objects are "amendment" or "inflicting pain," whose province is "morals and manners" or "faults and foibles," and whose audience is the "self-satisfied" or "the bystander." The Trudeau function, on the other hand, is more what Fowler defines as humor and wit, whose objects are "discovery" and "throwing light," whose province is "human nature" or "words and ideas," and whose audience is "the sympathetic" and "intelligent."

Furthermore, satire and sarcasm are defined as having "accentuation" or "inversion" as their method, while humor and wit are defined as employing "observation" or "surprise," and Trudeau's powers of observation are nearly unlimited. Who else could show us a rock superstar who is surprisingly, touchingly knocked out by his wife's pregnancy and the birth of their first child? Or the upper-class, bird-watching husband of Lacey Davenport, who survives the obscenity of being a Congressional spouse in Washington, and who for thirty-five years has been in his wife's words "the most interesting man at any party."

Those subleties are worthy of the best novel; yet Trudeau packs them all into a few lines of dialogue and into even fewer drawings. *Doonesbury* shows us a life that is all the clearer for being compressed. It brings us an imaginary garden that unites a whole world of disparate toads.

By allowing us to smile *with* characters rather than *at* them, Trudeau also allows us to admit just how like one or more of these characters we may be.

That's the fourth and best reason for reading this book. Where else can you smile while growing and learning?

THE HUMAN BRAIN. ONE OF LIFE'S GREATEST MIRACLES. STAGING AREA FOR THE 1,000,000 CHEMICAL REACTIONS A MINUTE THAT SHAPE HUMAN RESPONSES, RESPONSES WHICH IN SOME CASES AFFECT THE OUTCOME OF HISTORY ITSELF.

GOOD EVENING. FOR FOUR YEARS NOW, WE HAVE HAD THE CHANCE TO WATCH JIMMY CARTER'S MIND AT WORK. BUT WHAT OF RONALD REAGAN'S MIND? WHAT DO WE KNOW ABOUT IT? DOES SCIENCE REALLY KNOW WHAT MAKES HIM TICK?

I'M ROLAND HEDLEY. JOIN ME TONIGHT AS ABC UP-CLOSE NEWS TAKES A JOURNEY INTO THE UNKNOWN — A FANTASTIC VOYAGE THROUGH..THE BRAIN OF RONALD REAGAN!

"REAGAN'S BRAIN", BROUGHT TO YOU BY ANACIN..

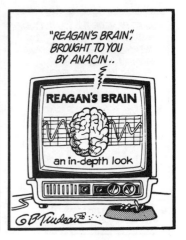

HI! WELCOME TO THE MYSTERIOUS WORLD OF RONALD REAGAN'S BRAIN! HOME OF NEARLY 30 BILLION NEURONS, OR "MARBLES," AS THEY ARE KNOWN TO THE LAYMAN!

WHAT WONDERS AWAIT US! THE FORNIX- REAGAN'S MEMORY VAULT, STOREHOUSE OF IMAGES OF AN IDYLLIC AMERICA, WITH 5¢ COKES, BURMA SHAVE SIGNS, AND HARDWORKING WHITE PEOPLE!

THE HYPOTHALAMUS, THE DEEP, DARK COILS OF HUMAN AGGRESSION, SOURCE OF REAGAN'S IMPULSES TO SEND U.S. FORCES TO ANGOLA, IRAN, KOREA, CYPRUS, CUBA, LEBANON AND COUNTLESS OTHER HOT SPOTS!

SO FASTEN YOUR SEAT BELTS! IT'S A TOPSY-TURVY FUNHOUSE OF A TRIP, BUT YOU WON'T BE SORRY! NOW THIS.

FIRST STOP, THE LEFT HEMISPHERE OF REAGAN'S CEREBRUM. TRADITIONALLY, THIS IS THE HOME OF LOGIC, ANALYSIS AND CRITICAL THINKING. LET'S TAKE A CLOSER LOOK..

AS YOU CAN SEE, MANY NERVES IN THIS PART OF THE BRAIN ARE FRAYED. THE RIGORS OF THE CAMPAIGN TRAIL, PARTICULARLY THE LACK OF SLEEP, HAVE TAKEN THEIR TOLL.

STUDIES HAVE SHOWN THAT SUBJECTS NOT ALLOWED TO SLEEP AND DREAM BECOME HIGHLY DISTURBED. THE BRAIN NEEDS TO DREAM; IF DEPRIVED AT NIGHT, IT COMPENSATES BY HALLUCINATING DURING THE DAY.

SEEN IN THIS LIGHT, MR. REAGAN'S ABILITY TO RECONCILE HUGE TAX CUTS WITH MASSIVE MILITARY SPENDING MUST BE VIEWED WITH SOME SYMPATHY.

REAGAN'S CEREBELLUM. HERE WE ENCOUNTER A MAZE OF NEURONS AND THEIR DENDRITIC SPINES, FROM WHOSE TIPS INFORMATION IS TRANSMITTED BY ELECTRICAL IMPULSES.

INTELLIGENCE IS THOUGHT TO BE RELATED TO THE COMPLEXITY OF THESE CONNECTIONS. UNHAPPILY, THE BRAIN STOPS GROWING AT AGE 20, AND THEREAFTER, NEURONS DIE OFF BY THE MILLIONS EVERY YEAR.

WHAT THIS MEANS IS THAT THE BRAIN OF RONALD REAGAN HAS BEEN SHRINKING EVER SINCE 1931, WHEREAS JIMMY CARTER'S BRAIN CELLS HAVE ONLY BEEN DYING SINCE 1944.

TO THE TRAINED SCIENTIST, THIS REPRESENTS A CLEAR CHOICE. BACK AFTER THIS.

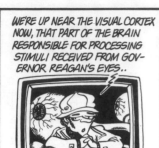

OKAY, LET'S GET DOWN TO CASES, DR. DAN. WHAT EXACTLY *IS* A "MELLOW MORTGAGE"?

A MELLOW MORTGAGE IS A SWEET DEAL, MARK..

THAT MEANS A LONG-TERM AGREEMENT WITH A LOW INTEREST RATE AND A SMALL DOWN PAYMENT. IT'S NOT EASY GETTING THESE TERMS, BUT ONCE YOU DO, YOU'RE ON YOUR WAY!

IN MY BOOK, I SHARE MY SECRETS, THE AMAZING TECHNIQUES WHICH CAN PARLAY A MERE $1000 INVESTMENT INTO A SPRAWLING, MULTIMILLION-DOLLAR EMPIRE IN A MATTER OF DAYS!

AND ALL YOU WANT IS $12.95? THAT HARDLY SEEMS FAIR.

IT'S AN INCREDIBLE OFFER, ISN'T IT?

DR. DAN, I WONDER IF YOU COULD EXPLAIN TO OUR LISTENERS WHAT "GENTRIFICATION" MEANS..

FOR SURE. IT WORKS LIKE THIS: A DEVELOPER BUYS A DILAPIDATED HOUSE IN A DEPRESSED NEIGHBORHOOD..

HE FIXES IT UP AND RESELLS IT TO A YOUNG, MIDDLE-CLASS COUPLE. THIS ENCOURAGES OTHER "GENTRY" TO BUY INTO THE NEIGHBORHOOD, AND BEFORE LONG, A FANTASTIC REAL ESTATE MARKET BOOMS WHERE NONE EXISTED BEFORE!

AND WHAT HAPPENS TO THE LOW-INCOME TENANTS WHO ARE DISPLACED? DOES ANYONE CARE?

SURE, WE DO. THESE PEOPLE ARE VERY IMPORTANT TO THE WHOLE PROCESS!

THEY ARE?

OF COURSE. THEY MOVE ON TO DEVALUE OTHER PROPERTIES. WITHOUT THEM, THE WHOLE SYSTEM FALLS APART.

DR. DAN, LET ME SEE IF I'VE GOT THIS STRAIGHT. WHAT YOU'RE SAYING IS THAT THE BEST REAL ESTATE INVESTMENTS ARE IN DECAYING NEIGHBORHOODS.

THAT'S RIGHT..

OF COURSE, SOME NEIGHBORHOODS PROVE VERY RESILIENT, SO IT'S OFTEN NECESSARY TO STIMULATE THE AREA'S DECLINE IN ORDER TO BRING DOWN LOCAL PROPERTY VALUES.

HOW DO YOU DO THAT?

NOTHING HEAVY-HANDED. WE MIGHT, FOR INSTANCE, DISTRIBUTE SPRAY PAINT AND CROW BARS TO THE LOCAL KIDS.

YOU GET THEM TO VANDALIZE THEIR OWN *HOMES*?

WELL, WITHIN LIMITS. WE ASK THEM NOT TO TOUCH THE COPPER PLUMBING.

WHO WAS THAT ON THE PHONE, HONEY?

IT WAS SUZY FROM DOWNSTAIRS. SHE'S BRINGING UP A TELEGRAM FOR ME!

A TELEGRAM? FROM WHOM?

MY GUESS IS IT'S FROM PEKING. THE GANG OF FOUR TRIAL IS ABOUT TO START, AND I'M SURE TO BE CALLED AS A KEY WITNESS.

WHY YOU, HONEY?

WELL, I USED TO BE MAO'S PERSONAL TRANSLATOR. AFTER HIS STROKE, I WAS THE ONLY PERSON IN CHINA WHO COULD UNDERSTAND HIM.

WOW.. SO DID HE REALLY ORDER THE CULTURAL REVOLUTION?

WELL, I THOUGHT SO, BUT I MAY HAVE GOTTEN IT WRONG.

MISS HUAN? I'M COMRADE ZHAO, FROM THE PROSECUTOR'S OFFICE. I'M GOING TO BE BRIEFING YOU ON YOUR TESTIMONY FOR THE TRIAL.

NICE TO MEET YOU, COMRADE. HOW'S THE TRIAL PROGRESSING?

SO FAR, VERY WELL.

THE STATE HAS CLEARLY ESTABLISHED THAT THE GANG OF FOUR IS GUILTY OF GENOCIDE IN THE DEATHS OF 34,375 INNOCENT PEOPLE. THE DEFENSE IS CLAIMING MANSLAUGHTER.

MAN-SLAUGHTER?

THEY SAY IT WAS 34,375 UNRELATED ACTS OF PASSION.

ARE ALL FOUR MEMBERS OF THE GANG BEING TRIED TOGETHER, COMRADE?

YES. ACTUALLY, THERE ARE TEN DEFENDANTS.

THE OTHERS ARE FROM THE CLIQUE OF SIX, A BAND OF REACTIONARY TRAITORS WHO PLOTTED TO ASSASSINATE THE CHAIRMAN IN 1971.

IT'S BEEN QUITE A YEAR FOR OUR NEW LEGAL SYSTEM. ALREADY THIS YEAR, WE'VE PROSECUTED THE MOB OF EIGHT, THE COW-DUNG SIX, THE NEST OF THREE, AND THE FOUR VERMIN.

YOU NAIL THEM ALL?

ALMOST. THE FOUR VERMIN SKIPPED BAIL.

SO HOW'S THE NEW CRIMINAL CODE BEEN WORKING OUT, COMRADE?

WELL, IT'S TAKEN SOME GETTING USED TO..

THE NEW ARTICLES PROVIDE FOR THE PRINCIPLE OF PUBLIC TRIAL AND THE RIGHT TO HIRE COUNSEL. THEY ALSO REQUIRE LIMITED DETENTION AND THE USE OF WARRANTS.

ALL THESE NEW RIGHTS HAVE CREATED CONSIDERABLE CONFUSION. FOR INSTANCE, JUST RECENTLY, "THE STATE VS. THE FIVE COCKROACHES" WAS THROWN OUT ON A TECHNICALITY.

NO KIDDING? WHAT SORT OF TECHNICALITY?

SCHEDULING ERROR. TURNED OUT THEY'D ALREADY BEEN EXECUTED.

COMRADE, ABOUT YOUR TESTIMONY. I DON'T HAVE TO TELL YOU HOW IMPORTANT IT IS THAT THE NAME OF THE GREAT HELMSMAN NOT BE DRAGGED THROUGH THE MUD..

AS HIS INTERPRETER, YOU WERE IN A UNIQUE POSITION TO KNOW IF THE CHAIRMAN REALLY ORDERED THE MURDEROUS EXCESSES OF THE CULTURAL REVOLUTION, AS HIS WIFE CONTENDS.

UH-HUH. WELL, YOU KNOW, COMRADE, THE CULTURAL REVOLUTION WAS SOMETHING OF AN OBSESSION WITH MAO..

YOU MEAN, WITH THE GANG OF FOUR.

RIGHT. DID I SAY MAO? I MEANT THE GANG OF FOUR.

I KNOW YOU DID. THAT'S WHY WE'RE HAVING THIS LITTLE CHAT.

WELL, I THINK THAT ABOUT COVERS IT, COMRADE. WE LOOK FORWARD TO YOUR TESTIMONY IN COURT TOMORROW.

THE GANG OF FOUR HAS COMMITTED TOWERING, MONSTROUS CRIMES. THE BLOOD OF THE CULTURAL REVOLUTION WILL BE ON THEIR HEADS FOREVER.

COMRADE, BETWEEN YOU AND ME, THE GANG OBVIOUSLY HAD A LITTLE HELP. WON'T YOU HAVE TO TRY THOUSANDS OF OTHERS, TOO?

"A SERPENT MAY BE A HUNDRED FEET LONG, YET TO KILL IT, ONLY THE HEAD MUST BE CUT OFF."

NICE. THAT BY MAO?

NO, SOME FACTORY WORKER. WE HAD A CONTEST.

WILL THERE BE MANY PEOPLE AT THE TRIAL, COMRADE?

YES, NEARLY 800 SPECTATORS, IN ADDITION TO THE 35 JUDGES.

35? WHY SO MANY?

AS A SAFEGUARD. WE WANT TO MAKE SURE THERE AREN'T ANY PROCEDURAL MISTAKES..

REMEMBER, MISS HUAN, WE HAVEN'T HAD A REAL LEGAL SYSTEM FOR 30 YEARS. THE WHOLE WORLD WILL BE WATCHING. THE TRIAL OF THE GANG OF FOUR MUST BE JUST AND SWIFT.

THEN WHY THE FOUR-YEAR DELAY?

WE HAD TO GET ALL THE JUDGES THROUGH LAW SCHOOL.

ISN'T HONEY GOING TO BE JOINING US TONIGHT, J.J.?

OH, DIDN'T I TELL YOU? SHE'S BACK IN PEKING.

REALLY? YOU MEAN FOR THE HOLIDAYS?

NO, FOR THE GANG OF FOUR TRIAL..

PRETTY AMAZING, HUH? IT TURNS OUT THAT MY ROOMMATE IS THE GOVERNMENT'S STAR WITNESS IN THE CASE AGAINST MADAME MAO!

THAT'S HER! THAT'S THE MAGGOT!

YOU'RE QUITE SURE, COMRADE?

MISS HUAN, AS MAO'S PERSONAL INTERPRETER, YOU WERE PRESENT DURING HIS WIFE'S SYSTEMATIC PERSECUTION OF ARTISTS AND INTELLECTUALS DURING THE CULTURAL REVOLUTION, WERE YOU NOT?

YES, THAT'S RIGHT.

I WONDER IF YOU COULD TELL THE COURT HOW MANY FATAL PERSECUTIONS YOU PERSONALLY WITNESSED, MISS HUAN.

WELL, LET'S SEE. THERE MUST HAVE BEEN AT LEAST 50, 60, SOMEWHERE IN THAT NEIGHBORHOOD.

THINK HARDER, MISS HUAN. WASN'T IT CLOSER TO 34,000?

WHY..YES! I REMEMBER NOW! THANK YOU, COMRADE.

NOT AT ALL. I COULD SEE YOU WERE BLOCKING.

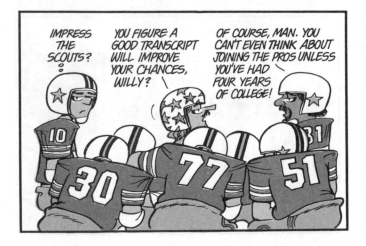

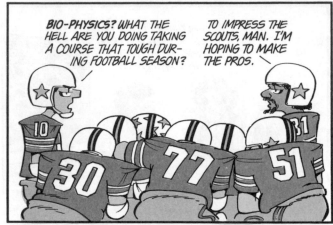

RICK! BOSS LADY ON LINE THREE!

YES, MRS. GRAHAM?

RICHARD, DEAR, I JUST WANTED TO MAKE SURE YOU'D BE GOING TO GEORGE WILL'S LITTLE FÊTE FOR THE REAGANS..

UH.. WELL, I..

WE'RE ALL SO PROUD OF GEORGE. AFTER FOUR YEARS OF THOSE DREARY CARTERS, I THINK IT'S WONDERFUL THAT ONE OF MY COLUMNISTS IS SEEING THAT THE REAGANS GET TO MEET ALL THE RIGHT PEOPLE!

YES, MA'AM. IT'S A DIRTY JOB, BUT SOMEBODY..

YOU WILL COVER IT FOR US, WON'T YOU, DEAR? GEORGE ISN'T GOING TO HAVE TIME.

MR. WILL? THIS IS RICK REDFERN. THE PAPER HAS ASKED ME TO DO A PIECE ON YOUR DINNER FOR THE REAGANS TONIGHT..

PLEASE, RICK, CALL ME GEORGE. I'M JUST A FELLA WHO WRITES COLUMNS LIKE YOURSELF.

UH.. OKAY, GEORGE. I WONDER IF YOU COULD TELL ME IF YOU'RE PLANNING ANYTHING SPECIAL..

OF COURSE NOT. IT'S JUST A QUIET GATHERING TO INTRODUCE THE REAGANS TO A FEW SHAKERS AND MOVERS.

LOOK, RICK, I'M NOT AN INTIMATE OF THE REAGANS. I'M NOT EVEN AN ADVISOR. I'M JUST A GUY FROM CHEVY CHASE WHO LIKES TO CHOW DOWN AND CHEW THE FAT WITH THE PRESIDENT-ELECT!

GOT IT. OKAY, LAST TIME, YOU HAD PINK TABLE CLOTHS. ANY CHANGE?

HEY, C'MON, THOSE WERE JUST OFF-THE-RACK ADOLFOS!

YOU KNOW WHAT HIS PROBLEM IS, DON'T YOU? REAGAN WON. NOW GEORGE THINKS HE'S A PROPHET.

SO WHO SAYS HE HAS TO BE A PROPHET WITH HONOR? IF MR. WILL WANTS TO JOIN THE RULING CLASS, THAT'S HIS PROBLEM, NOT YOURS!

YEAH.. YEAH, I GUESS YOU'RE RIGHT..

>SIGH<..

IT'S TOUGH BEING PURE.

ESPECIALLY IN YOUR UNDERWEAR.

MAY I TAKE YOUR COAT, MADAM?

THANK YOU. COULD YOU TELL ME WHERE I MIGHT FIND THE POWDER ROOM?

THAT WOULD BE DOWN THE HALL TO THE LEFT, MADAM.

MADAM WILL BE RIGHT BACK!

EXCUSE ME, SIR, ARE YOU BY ANY CHANCE MR. REDFERN?

YES, THAT'S RIGHT.

MR. WILL ASKED ME TO TELL YOU THAT HE DOESN'T NORMALLY HAVE A BUTLER.

I UNDERSTAND. MUM'S THE WORD.

GENERAL HAIG, I'M SURE YOU'RE AS ANXIOUS AS WE ARE TO BRING THESE HEARINGS TO A CONCLUSION..

SPEAKING FOR THE DEMOCRATIC MINORITY OF THE COMMITTEE, I CAN ASSURE YOU THAT WE ARE NOT INTERESTED IN DWELLING ON YOUR ROLE IN WATERGATE ANY LONGER THAN NECESSARY.

WELL, THANKS, SENATOR, BUT FRANKLY, I CAN HACK IT WITHOUT ANYBODY PULLING PUNCHES. WE'RE HERE TO DETERMINE MY FITNESS, SO STOP WHIMPERING AND GIVE ME YOUR BEST SHOT!

OH..UM..OKAY, WHAT WAS YOUR ROLE?

NONE OF YOUR DAMN BUSINESS!

GENERAL, WHEN YOU BECAME NIXON'S CHIEF OF STAFF DURING THE WATERGATE CRISIS, WHAT DID YOU HOPE TO ACCOMPLISH?

AS I'VE ALREADY INDICATED, I SOUGHT TO PRESERVE THE CONSTITUTION.

ARE YOU SERIOUS? FIGHTING TO WITHHOLD EVIDENCE, ADVISING NIXON TO LIE, ORDERING THE SPECIAL PROSECUTOR FIRED—ALL THAT WAS TO PRESERVE THE CONSTITUTION?

AFFIRMATIVE.

=SIGH..=

GENERAL, IF YOU'RE CONFIRMED, DO YOU EXPECT TO BE DOING THE CONSTITUTION ANY FURTHER FAVORS?

NOT AT THIS POINT IN TIME.

GENERAL HAIG, I WONDER IF WE MIGHT TURN OUR ATTENTION NOW TO THE QUESTION OF THE NIXON PARDON.

ACCORDING TO PUBLISHED ACCOUNTS, YOU DISCUSSED THE PARDON WITH MR. FORD ON AUGUST 1, 1974, AGAIN LATER THAT NIGHT, AND ONCE MORE ON AUGUST 2. CORRECT?

YES, BUT THERE WAS NEVER ACTUALLY A QUID PRO QUO OFFER. I WAS SIMPLY DESCRIBING ONE POSSIBLE SCENARIO.

AND MR. FORD'S REACTION? HE WAS APPALLED ALL THREE TIMES.

MOVING RIGHT ALONG, GENERAL, WE FIND THAT ANOTHER ONE OF YOUR CELEBRATED "MISSIONS" WAS DELIVERING TO THE FBI MR. KISSINGER'S REQUESTS FOR WIRETAPS ON HIS OWN STAFF..

MAY I ASSUME, GENERAL, THIS IS JUST ONE MORE STAIN OF WHICH YOU ARE ACTUALLY PROUD?

YOU MAY, SENATOR.

WE WERE FACED WITH A SECURITY CRISIS. OUR OPERATIONS WERE BEING COMPROMISED, SO ANYONE IN A POSITION TO KNOW ABOUT THE SECRET BOMBINGS IN CAMBODIA WAS SUSPECT. MY ONLY REGRET IS WE FAILED TO FIND ANY OF THE TRAITORS.

MAYBE IT WAS LEAKED BY THE VICTIMS.

WELL, WE THOUGHT OF THAT, BUT WE HAD NO LEGAL AUTHORITY TO PLACE TAPS IN CAMBODIA.

LET'S GO BACK TO THE BEGINNING OF YOUR CAPTIVITY, SHALL WE, MR. DUKE? AT LAST REPORT YOU WERE FACING A PREDAWN FIRING SQUAD.

RIGHT. AT THAT POINT, NEGOTIATIONS HAD KIND OF BOGGED DOWN. I WAS FORCED TO MAKE A LAST-DITCH OFFER OF $250,000, WHICH IT TURNED OUT WAS THE GOING RATE FOR A STAY OF EXECUTION.

IT WAS AN INCREDIBLE RIP-OFF, BUT I FIGURED, WHAT THE HELL, I'D BE LONG GONE BY THE TIME MY CHECK BOUNCED. UNFORTUNATELY, THEY LOCKED ME UP IN A HOTEL AS INSURANCE.

OKAY, BALD ONE, BACK TO THE ROOF.

I CAN'T UNDERSTAND IT. THEY MUST HAVE FROZEN MY ASSETS.

OKAY, BALD ONE, BACK TO THE ROOF.

LOOK, FELLAHS, I REALLY THINK YOU'RE OVERREACTING. WHY RISK WAR WITH THE U.S. OVER ONE LOUSY BAD CHECK?

I MEAN, IF YOU'RE SO BENT ON CREATING AN INTERNATIONAL INCIDENT, WHY DON'T YOU JUST SEIZE THE WHOLE UNITED STATES EMBASSY?

YOU SAID WHAT?

I WAS JUST KIDDING, FOR GOD'S SAKE..

THE NEXT DAY ALL HELL BROKE LOOSE..

THE EMBASSY'S BEEN SEIZED!

HUH?

IT'S YOUR LUCKY DAY, BALD ONE. WE'VE BEEN TOLD TO KEEP YOU ALIVE AS A BARGAINING CHIP!

GOOD PLAN. YOU WON'T REGRET IT.

SO WHAT DO YOU WANT TO DO WHILE THEY NEGOTIATE?

I DUNNO. WHY DON'T WE GO GRAB A BEER?

THE MONTHS DRAGGED BY..

GUARD!

KEEP IT DOWN, BALD ONE! I'M BUSY!

I THOUGHT YOU WERE GOING TO GET ME SOME CIGARETTES!

I SAID, QUIET! I'M TRYING TO STUDY!

WHAT DO YOU MEAN QUIET? I NEED THOSE CIGARETTES NOW! AND WHERE'S THAT NEW PICTURE? I'M SICK OF THIS DAMN ICON! DO YOU HEAR ME, GUARD?

FOR CRYING OUT LOUD, BALD ONE! I'VE GOT FINALS TOMORROW!

GET ME SOMETHING CLASSY, OKAY? YOU KNOW, LIKE A LEROY NEIMAN SPORTING PRINT!

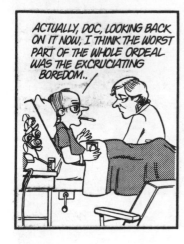

ACTUALLY, DOC, LOOKING BACK ON IT NOW, I THINK THE WORST PART OF THE WHOLE ORDEAL WAS THE EXCRUCIATING BOREDOM..

TO KEEP MYSELF ENTERTAINED, I USED TO FEIGN VARIOUS DISEASES DURING THE MEDICAL CHECK-UPS. THE DOCTOR WOULD INVARIABLY PRESCRIBE SOMETHING AND I'D SAVE IT.

THEN, EVERY SIX WEEKS OR SO, I'D HAVE A PARTY. IT NEVER FAILED TO SCARE THE HELL OUT OF THE GUARDS.

IS HE DEAD?

I DON'T THINK SO. HE JUST GIGGLED.

DOCTOR, WHAT SORT OF CONDITION IS THE 53RD HOSTAGE IN?

PHYSICALLY, HE SEEMS TO BE FINE..

PSYCHOLOGICALLY, THERE APPEAR TO BE SOME PROBLEMS. WHAT IS NOT CLEAR, HOWEVER, IS HOW MANY OF THEM EXISTED PRIOR TO HIS CAPTIVITY.

DOC, HAS HE CALLED HIS FAMILY YET?

AS A MATTER OF FACT, I THINK HE WAS PLANNING ON PHONING HIS LOVED ONES THIS MORNING..

$1000 ON OAKLAND, GOT IT?

DUKE, THE GAME WAS TWO WEEKS AGO. WHERE YOU BEEN?

I CAN LEAVE? HOT DAMN! WHEN?

TOMORROW. I SEE NO REASON TO KEEP YOU ANY LONGER.

I MUST WARN YOU, THOUGH. YOUR WORST ORDEAL MAY YET LIE AHEAD. YOU HAVE STILL TO FACE THE PRESS.

IT MIGHT BE A LITTLE ROUGH AT FIRST. HOSTAGES ARE REPORTING FEELINGS OF PARANOIA. MANY HAVE BEEN UNABLE TO GO TO THE BATHROOM WITHOUT BEING FOLLOWED BY A CAMERA CREW.

ARE THEY BEING MISTREATED?

ONLY BY A FEW FANATICS. MOSTLY LOCAL ANCHORMEN.

WELL, TODAY'S THE BIG DAY, MR. DUKE! HOW'S IT FEEL TO BE GOING HOME A HERO?

HERO? I'M A HERO?

YOU BETTER BELIEVE IT. THE RETURN OF THE HOSTAGES HAS PRODUCED AN INCREDIBLE OUTPOURING OF GOOD FEELING BACK HOME.

YOU'LL BE INVITED TO THE WHITE HOUSE, GIVEN PARADES, FREE BASEBALL TICKETS, FREE MEALS, FREE JEANS, YOU NAME IT! ALL YOU HAVE TO DO IS SHOW YOUR FORMER HOSTAGE I.D. CARD!

MY WHAT?

IT'S GOOD FOR UP TO 50% DISCOUNTS IN YOUR HOMETOWN.

LOOK, DAD, IF YOU ASKED ME TO COME HOME JUST SO YOU COULD GLOAT, I THINK I'LL BE ON MY..

CAN'T TAKE IT, HUH? THE KID WHO GLOATED OVER WATERGATE FOR FIVE YEARS?

YEAH, WELL, WHO CACKLED WITH GLEE WHEN NIXON BEAT MCGOVERN?

WHO BECAME INSUFFERABLE OVER VIETNAMIZATION?

THAT WASN'T AS BAD AS YOUR GLOATING OVER THE CAMBODIAN BLOODBATH!

ME? THAT WAS YOU!

IT WAS? ..YOU SURE?

UM.. I THINK SO. WHOSE FAULT DID THAT TURN OUT TO BE?

OFF TO WORK ALREADY, SWEETEST?

I'M AFRAID SO, DEAR. I HAVE TO GET READY FOR THE COMMITTEE'S HEARINGS ON THE NEW TAX CUTS TODAY.

WHAT A DREARY MESS THE WHITE HOUSE HAS HANDED US. IT'S NOTHING BUT ANOTHER WINDFALL FOR THE WEALTHY. AS IF THE RICH DIDN'T ALREADY HAVE ENOUGH WAYS TO AVOID PAYING TAXES!

WELL, GIVE THEM HECK, DEAR. BUT DO TRY TO KEEP IT IN PERSPECTIVE.

WHAT DO YOU MEAN, DICK?

DON'T FORGET WE'RE RICH.

DON'T WORRY, DEAR. I'LL TRY TO LEAVE IN A SAFETY NET.

WELL, I GUESS EVERYONE'S HERE. WHO'S OUR FIRST WITNESS TODAY, DEAR?

A MR. SLACKMEYER. HE JUST JOINED THE COUNCIL OF ECONOMIC ADVISERS.

REP. DAVENPORT

SLACKMEYER? HMM.. DON'T THINK I KNOW THAT NAME.

HE'S AN EXPERT IN TAX SHELTERS AND MONEY FUNDS.

HE LOOKS A LITTLE NERVOUS. HAS HE EVER TESTIFIED BEFORE?

YES. ONCE DURING THE TRUMAN ADMINISTRATION.

REP. DAVENPORT

POOR DEAR. I BETTER GO WARM HIM UP.

UM.. LACEY, TRY NOT TO GIVE AWAY THE QUESTIONS THIS TIME, OKAY?

REP. DAVENPORT

MR. SLACKMEYER? I'M MRS. DAVENPORT, AND I'D LIKE TO WELCOME YOU TO OUR LITTLE COMMITTEE HEARING..

OH.. WELL, THANK YOU, CONGRESSWOMAN.

WE'RE ALL LOOKING FORWARD TO YOUR TESTIMONY WITH SUCH INTEREST!

A FRIENDLY WORD OF WARNING, THOUGH. IF YOU INDULGE IN THE KIND OF METAPHYSICAL MUSH WE'VE BEEN HEARING FROM SO MANY OF YOUR COLLEAGUES LATELY, I CAN PROMISE YOU A VERY, VERY LONG AFTERNOON.

YOU CAN?

AFTERWARDS, OF COURSE, WE HOPE YOU'LL JOIN US FOR TEA AT MY OFFICE.

MADAM CHAIRWOMAN, IT IS WITH GREAT CONFIDENCE THAT I RECOMMEND TO THIS COMMITTEE THE ADMINISTRATION'S ECONOMIC RECOVERY PROGRAM.

I BELIEVE THAT IN THE VERY NEAR FUTURE, AMERICANS CAN EXPECT TO SEE AN ECONOMY IN WHICH INFLATION IS LOW, PRODUCTIVITY HIGH, THE FEDERAL BUDGET BALANCED, AND THE DOLLAR MIGHTY ONCE AGAIN!

HOW DO WE PROPOSE TO DO THIS? WELL, SIMPLY BY ADDING THREE ANNUAL TAX CUTS TO A TIGHT MONEY POLICY, A BURST OF DEREGULATION, A MASSIVE MILITARY BUILDUP, AND A SET OF CHANGING EXPECTATIONS.

TAKEN TOGETHER..

DON'T FORGET THE EYE OF A NEWT.

MR. SLACKMEYER, WOULDN'T YOU AGREE THAT THE MOST INDEFENSIBLE ASPECT OF YOUR TAX CUT PROPOSALS IS THE UNCONSCIONABLE WAY IN WHICH THEY FAVOR THE RICH?

NO, SIR, I CERTAINLY WOULD NOT. IF WE'RE GOING TO AVOID AN ECONOMIC ANZIO, THEN WE HAVE TO MOVE BOLDLY. WE CAN'T AFFORD TO ENGAGE IN A FISCAL BATTLE OF MIDWAY WITHOUT OUR CAPTAINS OF INDUSTRY!

FROM PAST EXPERIENCE, WE KNOW THAT THE WELL-HEELED ARE THE ONLY CLASS THAT CAN BE DEPENDED ON TO PUT THEIR TAX CUTS INTO SAVINGS AND INVESTMENTS!

AND THE POOR?

STUDIES SHOW THEY TEND TO BLOW IT ALL AT THE TRACK.

GOOD EVENING. TODAY THE FUROR CONTINUED OVER PRESIDENT REAGAN'S RECENT STATEMENT THAT THE ONLY LESSON OF VIETNAM WAS TO "NEVER ENTER INTO A WAR YOU DON'T INTEND TO WIN."

WITH THE MEMORY OF 210,000 U.S. CASUALTIES STILL VIVID, MILLIONS OF SHOCKED AMERICANS EXPRESSED OUTRAGE OVER THE DISCLOSURE THAT THEIR GOVERNMENT NEVER HAD ANY INTENTION OF WINNING THE VIETNAM WAR.

Vietnam 1959-1973

I'M ROLAND HEDLEY. AS CRIES OF "NEVER AGAIN" RING OUT ACROSS THE COUNTRY TONIGHT, JOIN ME AS WE TAKE A LOOK INTO OUR OWN FRONT YARD.. FOR A WAR WE CAN WIN!

BROUGHT TO YOU BY HERTZ, WHERE THE WINNERS RENT..

EL SALVADOR

ONE FOR THE GIPPER 1981-?

IN THE WAKE OF MR. REAGAN'S STARTLING DISCLOSURE THAT THE U.S. NEVER INTENDED TO WIN THE VIETNAM WAR, SCORES OF VETERANS HAVE COME FORWARD TO CONFIRM HIS CLAIM. SGT. LENNY MCCOVEY RECALLS.

VIETNAM

I REMEMBER ONCE NEAR DA NANG, WE HAD THIS GOOK UNIT PINNED DOWN IN THE OPEN. WE WERE ABOUT TO CALL IN SOME SKYRAIDERS FOR A NAPALM DROP WHEN THE C.O. JUST CALLED OFF THE OPERATION.

DID THAT HAPPEN OFTEN?

HELL, YES. EVERY TIME WE HAD A REAL CHANCE OF STICKING IT TO CHARLIE, WORD WOULD COME DOWN THE U.S. WASN'T SERIOUS ABOUT WINNING IN VIETNAM.

INCREDIBLE. HOW MANY OTHER G.I.'S KNEW ABOUT THIS?

PRETTY MUCH ALL 500,000 OF US.

WHETHER THE U.S. MEANT TO WIN THE VIETNAM WAR OR NOT, TODAY THERE IS GROWING PRESSURE TO FIND A WAR WE CAN WIN. U.S. STRATEGIST ABE LEVIN EXPLAINS HOW EL SALVADOR WAS SELECTED.

IT WASN'T EASY. WE'D BEEN LOOKING FOR A PLACE TO DRAW THE LINE FOR WEEKS, BUT THERE JUST WEREN'T ANY CIVIL WARS ON THE FRONT PAGE. FINALLY, SOME GUY IN RESEARCH HIT ON EL SALVADOR.

IT WAS PERFECT. SMALL, CLOSE TO HOME, AND THE RIGHT SIDE WAS ALREADY WINNING. WE HIT IT HARD. WITHIN DAYS, WE'D TURNED EL SALVADOR INTO A METAPHOR FOR THE GEOPOLITICAL STRUGGLE BETWEEN THE SUPERPOWERS!

AND THE RUS-SIANS AGREED WITH YOUR CHOICE?

WELL, NO, THEY WANTED SOME PERSIAN GULF STATE, BUT WE PUT OUR FOOT DOWN.

THE JUNTA. AN UNEASY COALITION OF CIVILIANS AND COMIC-OPERA COLONELS, HEADED, CURIOUSLY, BY A FORMER TORTURE VICTIM, JOSÉ DUARTE. RECENTLY I CHATTED WITH DUARTE ABOUT HIS TWO MISSING FINGERS.

MR. PRESIDENT, GIVEN THAT YOU YOURSELF WERE ONCE MUTILATED BY THE MILITARY, WHY ARE YOU WILLING TO DO BUSINESS WITH THEM?

WELL, IT TURNED OUT IT WAS ALL JUST A MISUNDER-STANDING.

BESIDES, MY PEOPLE LOVE ME FOR MY PAST SUFFERING. I AM ONE OF THEM. HAVING BEEN TO THE TORTURE CHAM-BERS, I KNOW WHAT IT'S LIKE TO LIVE IN THE SHADOW OF FEAR AND PAIN.

BUT ISN'T THAT REALLY JUST A POLITICAL GIMMICK, MR. PRESIDENT?

YOU'RE TOUGH, MY FRIEND.

EL SALVADOR. IS IT REAL-LY "ONE WE CAN WIN"? FURTHERMORE, WHAT CON-STITUTES WINNING? WITH HELP FROM AN INTERPRETER, WE TALKED TO SECRETARY OF STATE ALEXANDER HAIG..

SECRETARY HAIG, WHAT IS THE CHIEF U.S. OBJECTIVE IN EL SALVADOR TODAY?

TO IMPACT THE JUNTA MILITARILY, SO AS TO HEARTS-AND-MINDS THE INDIGENOUS ELEMENTS.

SECRETARY HAIG SAYS THE GOAL IS TO WIN LOCAL SUPPORT FOR THE JUNTA BY GIVING THEM MORE ARMS.

I SEE. AND HOW DO YOU PROPOSE TO GET CONGRES-SIONAL LEADERS TO GO ALONG WITH THIS?

WE PLAN TO SCENARIO THEM ROSILY.

SECRETARY HAIG SAYS..

I THINK I GOT IT.

HEY..

WHAT?

I THINK I JUST MADE A DECISION.

WHAT SORT OF DECISION?

I.. I THINK I WANT TO GET MARRIED.

THAT'S GREAT. TO WHOM?

NO, I'M SERIOUS. SOMETHING JUST CLICKED. GET YOUR COAT.

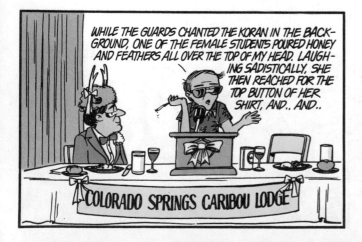

COMING UP:
THE EVENING
NEWS..

BUT FIRST, TELETYPE
MACHINE SOUND
EFFECTS! CLACKITY
CLACK!
CLACKITY..

GOOD EVENING. TODAY THE SENATE FINALLY
COMPLETED THE CONFIRMATION HEARINGS OF
CHESTER P. BIFFLE, NOMINEE FOR THE
POST OF DEPUTY SECRETARY OF STATE
FOR COLD WAR AFFAIRS.

THE HEARINGS HAD BEEN DELAYED WHILE A
FEDERAL GRAND JURY DELIBERATED EXTORTION
CHARGES AGAINST BIFFLE. ALTHOUGH HE WAS
FINALLY EXONERATED, THOSE CHARGES WERE
REPEATED TODAY BY SIX DIFFERENT WITNESSES.

OTHER WITNESSES ACCUSED BIFFLE OF CONFLICT
OF INTEREST, MOB CONNECTIONS, WAR CRIMES,
OBSTRUCTION OF JUSTICE AND SODOMY, BUT
IN SWORN TESTIMONY, FBI OFFICIALS CON-
FIRMED THAT BIFFLE WAS INNOCENT
UNTIL PROVEN GUILTY.

TURNING TO HIS QUALIFICATIONS, THE COMMITTEE
DETERMINED THAT BIFFLE'S FAMILIARITY WITH
FOREIGN AFFAIRS DID NOT EXTEND BEYOND HIS
SUBSCRIPTION TO "NATIONAL GEOGRAPHIC." HE
WAS UNABLE TO NAME THE LEADERS OF JAPAN,
FRANCE, GERMANY OR THE U.S.S.R.

HOWEVER, FOLLOWING BIFFLE'S TESTIMONY,
SENATOR JESSE HELMS PRAISED THE FORMER
REAGAN FUNDRAISER, SAYING, "NOBODY'S
GOT A MONOPOLY ON INTELLIGENCE OR VIR-
TUE." ADDED SENATOR CHARLES PERCY,
"HE SEEMS NICE ENOUGH."

BIFFLE'S CONFIRMATION
BY THE FULL SENATE
IS EXPECTED TOMORROW.   WHEW!

OKAY, LISTEN UP. TONIGHT'S PRESS CONFERENCE WILL BE AT 8:00 P.M.

BLACK TIE IS OPTIONAL.

I HOPE I'VE ANSWERED YOUR QUESTION, YOUNG LADY. WOULD YOU LIKE TO ASK A FOLLOW-UP?

OH, NO, THANK YOU, MR. PRESIDENT. I'D RATHER GIVE SOME OF THE OTHER GUYS A CHANCE.

WELL, THAT'S VERY GRACIOUS OF YOU. WHO'D LIKE TO GO NEXT? HOW ABOUT YOU, HOWARD?

THANK YOU, SIR, BUT I THINK ROGER HAD HIS HAND UP FIRST.

SO HE DID. ROGER?

THANK YOU, SIR. I'D LIKE TO ASK YOU IF YOU REALLY THINK IT'S POSSIBLE TO RECONCILE DEEP TAX CUTS, MASSIVE MILITARY SPENDING AND A BALANCED BUDGET WITHOUT HAVING TO USE DRUGS.

WELL..

HEY, C'MON, ROGER, THAT'S A VERY NEGATIVE QUESTION!

YEAH, ROGER, GIVE THE PRESIDENT'S POLICIES A FAIR CHANCE, FOR PETE'S SAKE!

THAT'S OKAY, BOYS, I'M A SKILLFUL COMMUNICATOR AND EDUCATOR. I CAN HANDLE IT.

GO TO IT, SIR! GOOD LUCK!

GOSH, HE'S UNFLAPPABLE.

BILL, THIS IS A NICKLE. AND THIS IS AN ORANGE. NOW, IF I GIVE YOU THE NICKLE, BUT I..

AH.. OPENING DAY..

THINK I'LL OVERDO IT.

SO HOW'S THE NEW TANNING SEASON SHAPING UP THIS YEAR, ZONK?

NOT SO GOOD, MARK. REAGAN'S NEW BUDGET CUTS HAVE THROWN THE WHOLE INDUSTRY INTO TURMOIL.

HOW SO?

THE NATIONAL ENDOWMENT FOR THE ARTS HAS BEEN FORCED TO CUT OFF ALL TANNING FELLOWSHIPS. NEARLY 1,000 APPRENTICE TANNISTS ARE GOING TO BE POUNDING THE SAND THIS SUMMER LOOKING FOR SPONSORS.

IT'S A SETBACK OF TRAGIC DIMENSIONS. IT'S NOT SO BAD FOR ESTABLISHED PROFESSIONALS LIKE MYSELF, WHO CAN FALL BACK ON ENDORSEMENTS AND COACHING, BUT IT'S A DISASTER FOR PEOPLE JUST BREAKING IN.

WHAT REAGAN'S DONE IS THROW A WHOLE GENERATION OF AMATEUR TANNISTS OUT ON THE BOARDWALKS. HUNDREDS OF MIDDLE-CLASS KIDS, WHO SAW TANNING AS A WAY OUT OF THE SUBURBS, WILL NOW PROBABLY TURN TO DRUGS OR BUSINESS SCHOOL!

WOW.. THAT'S AWFUL..

WHAT ABOUT PRIVATE FUNDING?

GEORGE HAMILTON'S ONLY ONE MAN. HE CAN'T DO THE JOB ALONE.

GBTrudeau

· LET THEM EAT ANECDOTES ·

YES, THIS IS ZONKER HARRIS.

MR. HARRIS, THIS IS NELSON COHN. I'M AN INVESTIGATIVE REPORTER FOR "TANNER'S WORLD."

"TANNER'S WORLD"? NO KIDDING?

YES, SIR. I'M CALLING ABOUT YOUR PRESS RELEASE, IN WHICH YOU CLAIM TO BE RETIRING BECAUSE OF YOUR "STUDIES"..

WELL, I'VE BEEN CHECKING AROUND, AND YOU HAVEN'T GONE TO CLASS IN MONTHS! YET YOU'RE RETIRING AT FAME'S DOORSTEP TO DEVOTE YOUR LIFE TO SCHOOL! IT DOESN'T ADD UP, MR. HARRIS. SOMETHING SMELLS, AND I'M GOING TO GET TO THE BOTTOM OF IT!

FANTASTIC! WHAT ISSUE WILL THIS BE IN?

IS IT THE MOB? IF YOU CAN'T TALK, JUST CLEAR YOUR THROAT.

IT JUST DOESN'T WASH, HARRIS. A WORLD-CLASS TANNIST DOESN'T RETIRE TO STUDY DENTISTRY!

OKAY, LOOK, I'LL LEVEL WITH YOU. IT WASN'T REALLY MY STUDIES..

THEN WHAT WAS IT? YOU HAD EVERYTHING GOING FOR YOU! YOU COULD HAVE HAD THE TITLE, YOU COULD HAVE BEATEN HAMILTON, YOU..

WHAT?

EXCUSE ME, MR. COHN, BUT ONE DOES NOT "BEAT" GEORGE HAMILTON! TAN-MASTER HAMILTON IS THE STANDARD AGAINST WHICH ALL OTHER TANS ARE MEASURED!

OH..SORRY.. I FORGOT YOU STUDIED UNDER HIM..

I THINK THIS CONVERSATION IS OVER, DON'T YOU?

YOU REALLY THINK ZONKER'S MAKING A BIG MISTAKE BY RETIRING, DON'T YOU, BERNIE?

DARN RIGHT I DO. IT'S JUST UNCONSCIONABLE. HE'S LETTING A LOT OF PEOPLE DOWN.

WELL, I WOULDN'T BE SO QUICK TO JUDGE, BERNIE. ZONKER'S PAID HIS DUES. HE SWEATED AND BAKED FOR FOUR YEARS OUT ON THAT CIRCUIT, AND HE WON A LOT OF NEW FANS FOR THE SEDENTARY ARTS.

I THINK HE'S ENTITLED TO A CHANGE NOW, BERNIE, AND HE'S ALSO ENTITLED TO OUR SUPPORT. HE'S GOT A BRAND-NEW LIFE AHEAD OF HIM, AND I ADMIRE HIS COURAGE FOR FACING IT SQUARELY!

..AND IT LOOKS LIKE ANOTHER CLEAR, SUNNY WEEKEND, JACK!

MY GOD.. WHAT HAVE I DONE?..

ZONKER, I KNOW HOW YOU MUST FEEL, I REALLY DO. IT CAN'T BE EASY GIVING UP YOUR LIFE'S WORK..

BUT YOU CAN'T SPEND THE REST OF YOUR LIFE IN A STATE OF PRE-CANCEROUS REPOSE. YOU HAVE TO MOVE ON, DEVELOP SOME NEW INTERESTS!

THERE'S NO SHAME IN IT, ZONKER! YOU HAVE TO STOP FEELING GUILTY! YOU HAVE TO STOP TEARING YOURSELF APART OVER THIS THING!

ZZZZ..

THAT'S IT. TRY TO GET SOME SLEEP.

'MORNING, GENTS!

LOOK WHO'S UP!

FEELING BETTER, ZONK?

LOADS, THANKS. IN FACT, IT MIGHT BE FAIR TO SAY I'M A NEW MAN!

I'VE BEEN THINKING A LOT ABOUT WHAT MIKE SAID, HOW I HAD TO PUT TANNING BEHIND ME, HOW I NEEDED TO DEVELOP A NEW INTEREST.

SETTLE ON ANYTHING YET?

I'VE NARROWED IT DOWN TO SPACE INVADERS AND GIRLS.

I'D GO WITH SPACE INVADERS.

RIGHT. AT LEAST UNTIL YOU GET YOUR SELF-CONFIDENCE BACK.

HIS ROYAL HIGHNESS, THE PRINCE OF WALES. FUTURE KING OF ENGLAND, KNIGHT OF THE GARTER, GREAT MASTER OF THE ORDER OF THE BATH, AND NERVOUS BRIDEGROOM.

MUNIR HASSAN, PAKISTANI IMMIGRANT. LIKE CHARLES, 32 AND UNEMPLOYED. UNLIKE THE PRINCE, ONE OF HUNDREDS OF INDIANS AND ASIANS WHO ROCKED THE SOUTHALL SECTION OF LONDON WITH A WEEK OF RIOTS!

GOOD EVENING. THIS IS ROBERT MACNEIL. WITH THE EMBERS STILL SMOLDERING FROM BRITAIN'S WORST RIOTING IN OVER A CENTURY, WE EXAMINE WHAT HAPPENS WHEN..

".. THE EMPIRE STRIKES BACK!"

MADE POSSIBLE BY GRANTS FROM THE PRIVATE SECTOR.

THE EMPIRE STRIKES BACK!

BRITAIN'S STICKY RIOTS

GOOD EVENING. I'M ROBERT MACNEIL. TONIGHT WE FOCUS ON BRITAIN'S RIOTS. I'LL BE ASKING SMOOTH, URBANE QUESTIONS FROM NEW YORK. JIM LEHRER WILL HANDLE THE EARNEST, PLAIN-SPOKEN QUESTIONS FROM WASHINGTON. JIM?

ROBIN, OUR FIRST GUEST IS INSPECTOR BLACKSTONE CALDECOTE-HAYDEN OF SCOTLAND YARD. INSPECTOR, WHAT WAS THE NATURE OF YOUR RECENT RIOTING? WAS RACE A MAJOR ISSUE?

RACE? YES, QUITE. SOME OF THE BROWN CHAPS DID HAVE A GO AT OUR LADS. BUT TO US, OF FAR GREATER DISTRESS WAS THAT THE HOOLIGANISM TOOK PLACE ON THE EVE OF CHARLES'S WEDDING.

DOES THE ROYAL FAMILY KNOW?

THEY'VE BEEN TOLD THERE WAS A SPOT OF UNPLEASANTNESS, YES.

LORD PENNINGTON CAMELOT-JONES, WE APPRECIATE YOUR TAKING TIME OUT FROM THE WEDDING TO CHAT WITH US..

NOT AT ALL, IT'S ALL A BIT TIRESOME ANYWAY, ISN'T IT?

YOUR LORDSHIP, WHAT WILL YOUR GOVERNMENT BE DOING TO PREVENT A RECURRENCE OF THE RECENT VIOLENCE?

WELL, I SHAN'T THINK WE'LL BE DOING ANY MORE PANDERING..

ENGLAND WILL STOP THE RABBLE IN THE STREET THE SAME WAY WE BEAT THE JERRYS — WITH STRONG LEADERSHIP!

YOUR LORDSHIP, I HAVE A QUESTION..

BLOODY GOOD. WHERE ARE YOU?

WASHINGTON. WHAT ABOUT JOBS?

AMONG THE RIOTERS WHO FOUGHT POLICE IN THE BLIGHTED TOXTETH DISTRICT OF LIVERPOOL WAS A 17-YEAR-OLD DROP-OUT WHO CALLS HIMSELF "TEDDY SPUTUM."

MR. SPUTUM, WHY DID YOU PERSONALLY PARTICIPATE IN THE RIOTS?

THE BLOODY COPPERS, MAN! WE HATE 'EM! THEY BEEN KNOCKIN' US ABOUT FOR YEARS SO WE GOT EVEN!

ALSO, THERE'S NO BLEEDIN' JOBS, IS THERE? WE GOT NUTHIN TO DO BUT HANG OUT! WITHOUT A JOB, I DON'T HAVE ME SELF-RESPECT!

I SEE. AND WHAT LINE OF WORK WERE YOU INTERESTED IN, MR. SPUTUM?

I DUNNO..MAYBE SOMETHIN' IN THE FASHION INDUSTRY.

MR. REGINALD NEWHALL-CADBURY, A DISTANT COUSIN OF THE EARL OF CADBURY, IS A SOLICITOR IN STRIFE-TORN LIVERPOOL. HE IS ALSO A CONVICTED RIOTER.

MR. NEWHALL-CADBURY, WHAT PROMPTED YOU TO JOIN THE LIVERPOOL RIOTS?

INDIGNATION, I SHOULD SAY. I WASN'T VERY KEEN ON THE ROYAL WEDDING VOWS.

LADY DIANA REFUSED TO TAKE THE TRADITIONAL VOW TO "OBEY" CHARLES. A PROPER LITTLE LIBBER, SHE WAS. I DIDN'T FANCY IT, AND I DARESAY A LOT OF OTHER BLOKES FELT LIKEWISE.

SO YOU THREW A BRICK IN PROTEST?

TWO, ACTUALLY. IT WAS ALL WE COULD SPARE FROM THE GARDEN.

PROFESSOR ARMSTRONG-FOOTE, IS IT FAIR TO SAY, THEN, THAT THE RIOTS WERE MOTIVATED AS MUCH BY HOOLIGANISM AS BY BLEAK ECONOMIC CONDITIONS?

YES, I THINK SO.

I SEE. ROBIN?

YES, PROFESSOR, WOULD YOU ALSO AGREE THAT THE REVERSE MIGHT BE TRUE?

UM.. YES, I GUESS I WOULD.

I SEE. JIM?

I SEE, TOO. ROBIN?

YOU GUYS SURE ARE EVEN-HANDED.

LESTER? HI, DUKE HERE..

DUKE! LONG TIME, BUDDY! HOW'S THE HOUSE COMING?

IT'S DONE. I TORE DOWN THAT HIPPIE WINDMILL BRENNER PUT UP AND REBUILT IT FROM SCRATCH.

WELL, CONGRATULATIONS!

THANKS. I WAS THINKING OF HAVING A LITTLE HOUSEWARMING PARTY. COULD YOU SEND OUT A DOZEN CASES OF WILD TURKEY?

SURE. HOW MANY GUESTS ARE YOU HAVING?

GUESTS?

IT'S CUSTOMARY. YOU GET A LOT MORE PRESENTS THAT WAY.

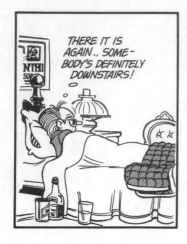
THERE IT IS AGAIN.. SOME-BODY'S DEFINITELY DOWNSTAIRS!

HMM.. I COULD BE WALKING INTO A TRAP.. I BETTER SHOOT FIRST, ASK QUESTIONS LATER..

BLAM! BLAM! BLAM! BLAM! BLAM!

HELLO? ANYONE THERE?

>GURGLE..<

ONE MOVE AND YOU'RE A DEAD MAN!

DUKE..DON'T SHOOT.. IT'S ME..>COUGH< BRENNER..

BRENNER! WHAT THE HELL ARE-YOU DOING HERE?

YOU.. >GASP< YOU..

WHOA.. I REALLY WINGED YOU GOOD, DIDN'T I? SORRY ABOUT THAT, KID.. ACCIDENTS HAPPEN..

YOU.. YOU TRIED TO KILL ME!

DON'T BE SILLY. I THOUGHT YOU WERE A RACCOON. WANT A BEER?

HERE..USE THIS TOWEL AS A TOURNIQUET.. YOU'RE BLEED-ING LIKE A STUCK PIG..

YOU.. >COUGH< YOU.. TRIED TO KILL ME, MAN..

WILL YOU GET OFF THAT, BRENNER? I TOLD YOU, I THOUGHT YOU WERE A RACCOON!

YOU TRIED TO MURDER ME, MAN..

WHY YOU PATHETIC LITTLE PUP! DO YOU REALLY THINK I WOULD JEOPARDIZE MY CAREER BY WASTING A PUNK LIKE YOU? DON'T FLATTER YOUR-SELF, JACK!

MURDERER.

LOOK, I GOTTA GET SOME SHUT-EYE. YOU WANT AN AMBU-LANCE OR WHAT?

PLEASE.

HEY, HOLD IT DOWN, WILLYA KID? I'M ON THE PHONE!

MUR-DERER!

GOOD EVENING, ASPEN AMBU-LANCE.

HELLO, LES? DUKE HERE. LOOK, WE'VE HAD A LIT-TLE ACCIDENT OUT AT THE HOUSE. BRENNER'S TAKEN A SLUG. HE'S BLEEDING ALL OVER THE PLACE.

OKAY, HOLD ON, DUKE. I'LL SEND A WAGON OUT RIGHT AWAY.

GOOD. LISTEN, LES, THIS IS KIND OF A SENSITIVE MATTER. I'M THINKING ABOUT GETTING BACK INTO POLITICS, SO I'D APPRECIATE YOUR DIS-CRETION.

I HEAR YOU, OL' BUDDY. I'LL HAVE THE GUYS USE THE BACK ROAD.

GREAT. SAY, COULD YOU HAVE THEM SWING BY AND PICK ME UP A PIZZA?

NO PROBLEM. YOU WANT IT WITH EVERY-THING?

IT WAS REALLY HIS OWN FAULT. I CAUGHT HIM BREAKING IN..

MAN, WHAT A MESS! WHAT'D YOU USE, DUKE, AN M-60?

ACCIDENTS HAPPEN, LEO. I HOPE I CAN TRUST YOU TO KEEP THIS LITTLE MISHAP TO YOURSELF..

HEY, HAVE WE EVER LET YOU DOWN BEFORE, DUKE?

REMEMBER THAT TIME I CAME OUT HERE AND PUMPED OUT THAT LADY'S STOMACH? YOU NEVER HEARD ANOTHER WORD ABOUT THAT, DID YOU?

I'M HEARING IT RIGHT NOW, LEO.

HEY, MAN, THIS DUDE'S UNCONSCIOUS. THAT'S GOING TO BE EXTRA.

PREP HIM RIGHT AWAY AND GET HIM INTO O.R.!

HOW BAD IS IT, DOC?

I WON'T KNOW UNTIL I OPEN HIM UP. WHAT HAPPENED?

IT WAS JUST SOME FREAK ACCIDENT. WILL HE MAKE IT?

IT COULD GO EITHER WAY. HE'S GOT A HOLE IN HIM THE SIZE OF A GRAPEFRUIT.

THAT'S TERRIBLE.. JUST TERRIBLE..

I'LL LET YOU KNOW IF IT'S HOMICIDE OR ASSAULT.

THANKS. I'LL BE OUT IN MY CAR, OKAY?

MR. DUKE?

YO?

I HAVE SOME GOOD NEWS FOR YOU, MR. DUKE..

BRENNER'S GOING TO MAKE IT?

HE IS INDEED. WE WERE ABLE TO STOP THE BLEEDING AND REMOVE THE BULLET.

OH, THANK GOD! BLESS YOU, DOCTOR!

MOM? GOOD NEWS! HE'S GOING TO BE OKAY!

SWISSAIR. THANK YOU FOR HOLDING.

GREAT TO HAVE YOU BACK, BRENNER. I WAS ROOTIN' FOR YOU.

SURE YOU WERE, DUKE..

EXCUSE ME, SON. ARE YOU ZEKE BRENNER?

HOLD IT, BUDDY. DIDN'T YOU SEE THE NO VISITORS SIGN?

DENVER POLICE. THE NAME'S LT. O'MALLEY.

POLICE? SOMEBODY SENT FOR THE POLICE?

YES, IT'S CUSTOMARY FOLLOWING A CRIME.

OH, NO.. DON'T TELL ME HE'S MIXED UP WITH DRUGS AGAIN!

HEY, WAIT A MINUTE..

THANKS FOR SPRINGING ME, HONEY. I WAS BEGINNING TO GO A LITTLE STIR-CRAZY IN THERE.

JAIL MUST BE ROUGH, SIR.

IT'S A LIVING HELL, HONEY, A STINKING PIT OF INHUMANITY WHICH ONLY THE STRONG SURVIVE.

GOSH.. IT SOUNDS AWFUL..

SO HOW LONG HAVE YOU BEEN WITHOUT A WOMAN, SIR?

SINCE FRIDAY. JUST DROP ME OFF AT THE BUS STATION, BUDDY.

WHERE DO YOU THINK WE OUGHT TO GO FOR OUR ANNUAL BIRDING OUTING THIS YEAR, THAD?

I'D SAY THE MATAGORDA ISLAND WILDLIFE REFUGE. BEFORE IT'S TOO LATE.

BEFORE IT'S TOO LATE?

SECRETARY WATT IS TRYING TO GIVE THE REFUGE BACK TO THE STATE OF TEXAS FOR DEVELOPMENT. IN A FEW YEARS, IT SHOULD LOOK LIKE CONEY ISLAND.

WHAT? WATT CAN'T DO THAT! THAT REFUGE IS HOME FOR MANY ENDANGERED SPECIES, INCLUDING THE BROWN PELICAN, THE SOUTHERN BALD EAGLE AND THE WHOOPING CRANE!

I KNOW, I KNOW..

DOES THE PRESIDENT KNOW ABOUT THIS?

AFRAID SO. HE'S GIVEN THEM UNTIL SEPTEMBER TO GET OUT.

..AND THAD SAYS THAT SECRETARY WATT HAS ALREADY APPROACHED TEXAS ABOUT TAKING BACK THE MATAGORDA WILDLIFE REFUGE!

THAT MEANS DEVELOPMENT, WHICH MEANS THE END OF AN UNDISTURBED HABITAT FOR SEVERAL DIFFERENT ENDANGERED SPECIES!

IT'S OUTRAGEOUS AND UNCONSCIONABLE! AS SECRETARY OF THE MARYLAND AUDUBON SOCIETY, I'M SERIOUSLY THINKING OF DEMANDING WATT'S RESIGNATION IN OUR NEXT NEWSLETTER!

WHY, DEAREST! YOU'VE BEEN POLITICIZED!

I HAVE NO CHOICE. PART OF HAVING CLOUT IS NOT BEING AFRAID TO USE IT!

AREN'T YOU GOING TO SLEEP, DEAR?

I'M TOO STEAMED TO SLEEP, LACEY.

IN ALL MY YEARS OF CONSERVATION WORK, I DON'T THINK I'VE EVER SEEN SUCH A RECKLESS AND ARROGANT PUBLIC SERVANT AS THIS MAN WATT!

I'LL TELL YOU ONE THING, I'M NOT SITTING IDLY BY TO WATCH THE GREATEST WILDLIFE REFUGE SYSTEM IN THE WORLD WANTONLY DISMANTLED! I'M TAKING THIS STRAIGHT TO MY CONGRESSMAN!

BUT, SWEETEST, I'M YOUR CONGRESSMAN.

YOU'LL BE HEARING FROM ME IN THE MORNING.

GOOD MORNING, SECRETARY WATT'S OFFICE.

YES, THIS IS RICHARD DAVENPORT. I'D LIKE TO SPEAK WITH THE SECRETARY, PLEASE.

WHAT WOULD THIS BE CONCERNING, SIR?

IT CONCERNS THE EXPLOITATION OF OUR WILDLIFE REFUGES.

I'M SORRY, SIR, THE SECRETARY ISN'T AVAILABLE TO SPEAK TO ENVIRONMENTAL EXTREMISTS.

BUT I'M A MODERATE!

OH, THAT'S DIFFERENT. WHAT OIL COMPANY ARE YOU WITH, SIR?

MR. SECRETARY? WHAT IS IT, MISS DEMPSEY?

SIR, YOU'VE BEEN GETTING CALLS ALL MORNING FROM AN IRATE BIRD WATCHER. HE'S UPSET ABOUT THE PROPOSED TRANSFER OF THE MATAGORDA REFUGE.

WHAT FOR?

HE CLAIMS IT COULD LEAD TO THE EXTINCTION OF FOUR DIFFERENT SPECIES OF NORTH AMERICAN BIRDS.

SO WHAT? WE'LL STILL HAVE MILLIONS OF PIGEONS! I RUN OVER 'EM IN THE PARKING LOT ALL THE TIME!

PIGEONS, SIR?

BIRDS ARE BIRDS, MISS DEMPSEY. THIS IS WHAT I MEAN BY EXTREMISM.

SO ANYWAY, I'VE DECIDED TO CALL AN EMERGENCY MEETING OF THE BOARD TO VOTE ON A DEMAND FOR JAMES WATT'S REMOVAL!

ARE YOU SERIOUS, DICK? YOU WANT TO THROW THE WHOLE WEIGHT OF THE MARYLAND AUDUBON SOCIETY BEHIND A CALL FOR WATT'S RESIGNATION?

THAT'S RIGHT, THAD.

DICK.. DICK, OL' MAN..

WHAT?

ISN'T THAT GOING AFTER THE PROBLEM WITH AN AWFULLY BIG STICK?

THESE ARE DRASTIC TIMES, CHUM OF MINE.

OH, THERE YOU ARE, DEAREST! WHERE'VE YOU BEEN?

I WAS OVER DISCUSSING STRATEGY WITH THADIUS.

YOU MEAN THE WILDLIFE REFUGE BUSINESS? DID YOU EVER GET HOLD OF WATT?

NOPE. I CALLED FIVE TIMES, BUT HIS ASSISTANT WOULDN'T PUT ME THROUGH.

WHY NOT?

SHE SAID MR. WATT HAD MORE IMPORTANT THINGS TO DO THAN TALK WITH THE SECRETARY OF THE MARYLAND AUDUBON SOCIETY!

A LIKELY STORY.

IT'S HER FUNERAL. I'VE CALLED AN EMERGENCY MEETING OF THE BOARD FOR TONIGHT.

GOOD EVENING. TODAY THE GOVERNORS OF FOUR NEW ENGLAND STATES ASKED FOR EMERGENCY FEDERAL AID TO HELP CONTROL GROWING INFESTATIONS OF THE AMERICAN PREPPY.

CITING THE THREAT OF QUARANTINE FROM NEIGHBORING STATES, THE FOUR GOVERNORS ANNOUNCED A JOINT PROGRAM TO COMBAT WHAT IS BEING REGARDED AS A PARTICULARLY VIRULENT STRAIN OF WASP.

GOVERNOR KING OF MASSACHUSETTS, WHOSE STATE IS HARDEST HIT, BLAMED THE NEW POLITICAL CLIMATE IN WASHINGTON FOR THE PROLIFERATION OF THESE PESKY ELITISTS.

AERIAL SPRAYING IS EXPECTED TO COMMENCE AT ONCE.

GOOD EVENING. TODAY IN WASHINGTON, A STORM OF CONTROVERSY WAS UNLEASHED BY THE NEWS THAT FOUR NEW ENGLAND GOVERNORS HAD DECIDED TO SPRAY LOCAL INFESTATIONS OF PREPPIES.

FUMED PREPPY STANDARD-BEARER GEORGE BUSH, "IT'S OUTRAGEOUS! THERE AREN'T EVEN THAT MANY PREPS IN NEW ENGLAND DURING THE OFF-SEASON. MOST OF US TIP WELL AND LEAVE BY LABOR DAY."

MEANWHILE, THE CAUSES OF THE PREP EXPLOSION ARE STILL UNDER INVESTIGATION, BUT PRELIMINARY FINDINGS SUGGEST THAT THE REAGANS' INFATUATION WITH THE WEALTHY AND SOCIALLY CONNECTED IS A MAJOR FACTOR.

WHITE HOUSE SPOKESWOMAN MUFFY BRANDON DISMISSED SUCH SPECULATION AS TACKY.

".. AND THE GOVERNOR NOTED THAT LIMITED AERIAL SPRAYING OVER PREPPY BREEDING GROUNDS LIKE GREENWICH, CONNECTICUT, HAD ONLY SERVED TO RAISE PROPERTY VALUES IN NEARBY WESTPORT."

BOY.. I HAD NO IDEA THE PREPPY PROBLEM HAD GOTTEN SO OUT OF HAND..

THE GOVERNOR'S DOING THE RIGHT THING. STATEWIDE SPRAYING IS THE ONLY SOLUTION.

"OTHER PROPOSALS, SUCH AS REFORMING THE INHERITANCE TAX LAWS OR SHUTTING DOWN SELECTED BOARDING SCHOOLS, WERE REJECTED AS TOO LIMITED TO IMPACT ON PREPPY POPULATIONS."

"STERILIZING MALE PREPS WAS ALSO VIEWED AS UNACCEPTABLE."

WHY?

TOO EXPENSIVE. THEY'D ALL WANT SPECIALISTS.

WE'RE BACK! I'M TALKING BY PHONE TO MR. LARRY CLEAVER, HEAD OF CONNECTICUT'S CONTROVERSIAL NEW PREPPY ERADICATION PROGRAM..

MR. CLEAVER, ASIDE FROM AERIAL SPRAYING, WILL YOU BE TAKING OTHER MEASURES TO CONTROL PREP POPULATIONS?

OH, MOST DEFINITELY, MARK..

WHAT WE'RE TRYING TO DO IS GET THE AVERAGE CITIZEN INVOLVED. TO THIS END, THE STATE WILL BE GRANTING TAX CREDITS TO ANYONE WHO TURNS IN SIX OR MORE ALLIGATOR SHIRTS.

PREPPY PELTS, AS IT WERE.

RIGHT. HOW HE GETS 'EM IS HIS BUSINESS.

MR. CLEAVER, I'M SURE MANY PEOPLE ARE WONDERING RIGHT NOW IF THERE ISN'T SOME LESS RADICAL WAY OF CONTROLLING THE SPREAD OF PREPPIES THAN AERIAL SPRAY- ING..

FOR INSTANCE, HAVE YOU CONSIDERED DISRUPTING THE REPRODUCTIVE CYCLE OF ADULT PREPPIES?

YES, BUT THE PROBLEM THERE IS THAT PREPPIES MATE SO RARELY, AND THEN ONLY ON THE ADVICE OF THEIR FAMILY ATTORNEYS.

HOW ABOUT CROSS-BREEDING THEM WITH HIGH SCHOOL GRADUATES?

WELL, WE'RE TRYING TO AVOID THAT KIND OF SOCIAL ENGINEERING.

VICE-PRESIDENT BUSH, DO YOU THINK THE NEW ESTATE LAWS HAVE CON- TRIBUTED TO THE CUR- RENT PREP EXPLOSION?

GOSH, I DON'T THINK SO. IN WHAT WAY?

WELL, SIR, WHEN OLD PREPS DIE OFF, THE NEW TAX LAWS NOW ALLOW BABY PREPPIES TO RETAIN THEIR FAMILY FORTUNES INTACT. ISN'T THIS JUST ONE MORE BREAK FOR THE WELL-HEELED?

LADIES AND GENTLEMEN, I HAVE ONLY ONE THING TO SAY TO YOU ON THE SUBJECT: THE GREATEST PREP OF THEM ALL, F. SCOTT FITZGERALD, DIED VIRTUALLY PENNILESS.

UM.. YOUR POINT BEING, SIR?

NEVER AGAIN.

MR. SLACKMEYER, I'M SURE YOU AND YOUR COLLEAGUES ON THE COUNCIL OF ECONOMIC ADVISORS ARE AWARE OF THE HIGHLY UNFAVORABLE MARKET RESPONSE TO REAGANOMICS..

OF COURSE, SIR.

AS A RECENT LEADER OF THE FINANCIAL COMMUNITY YOUR- SELF, CAN YOU THINK OF ANY REASON WHY WALL STREET SHOULD BE REACTING SO NEGATIVELY TO YOUR CURRENT POLICIES?

WELL, SENATOR, AS HARD AS IT IS FOR ME TO ACCEPT THE POSSIBILITY, I'M AFRAID WALL STREET'S HOSTILITY MAY BE..WELL, PERSONAL.

PERSONAL, MR. SLACK- MEYER?

LET'S JUST SAY I HAD A FEW HEADS BROUGHT TO ME IN MY DAY, SENATOR.

SENATOR, WHAT WE'RE SEEING NOW IS **RAMPANT** OPPORTUN- ISM! INVESTORS ARE TAKING ADVANTAGE OF HIGH INTEREST RATES TO SCORE BIG IN THE MONEY FUNDS!

IT'S A MARKET OF SHAME NOW, SENATOR. HELL, I DON'T **KNOW** THE PLACE ANYMORE! THE WALL STREET I KNEW WAS VIBRANT, VISIONARY, GUTSY, NOT NERVOUS, GREEDY AND SHORT-SIGHTED!

I'M **ASHAMED** TO HAVE EVER BEEN A FINANCIER! THESE PEOPLE DON'T CARE IF THE PRESIDENT'S PLAN SUCCEEDS! ALL WALL STREET'S INTER- ESTED IN IS **MAKING MONEY!**

UM.. WHICH IS, OF COURSE, ONE OF ITS NATURAL FUNCTIONS.

MANFULLY CONCEDED, SIR!

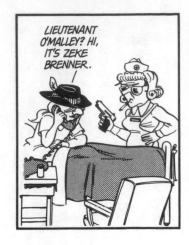

LOOK! OVER THERE! PARENTS FOR AS FAR AS THE EYE CAN SEE!

I HAD NO IDEA THERE WERE SO MANY STATION WAGONS STILL ON THE ROAD!

MAYBE YOU CAN RENT THEM JUST FOR GRADUATION.

..AND THE FINAL AWARD OF THE DAY IS, A PERSONAL FAVORITE, THE CLASS OF '70 MEMORIAL MAY DAY AWARD.

"THE CLASS OF '70 MEMORIAL MAY DAY AWARD IS GIVEN IN MEMORY OF THOSE STUDENTS WHO SERVED IN THE CAMPUS DEMONSTRATIONS OF THE SPRING OF 1970.."

"IT IS AWARDED EACH YEAR TO THAT SENIOR WHOSE LOVE OF WORLD PEACE, HUMAN RIGHTS, SOCIAL JUSTICE, AND GOOD ROCK AND ROLL BEST EXEMPLIFIES THOSE IDEALS ESPOUSED BY THE STUDENT MOVEMENT OF THE LATE SIXTIES."

FOR HIS OPPOSITION TO IMPERIALISM AND RACISM, FOR HIS SENSITIVITY TO THE PLIGHT OF THE URBAN POOR, AND FOR PUTTING SERVICE TO COMMUNITY ABOVE SELF-INTEREST, THE CLASS OF '70 AWARD IS GIVEN THIS YEAR TO.. ARTHUR P. PINSON!

BOOO! BOO!

DO-GOOD WEENIE!

HA, HA!

HA! HA!

HA, HA! I CAN'T BELIEVE THEY STILL GIVE THAT AWARD!

HIPPIE!

ARTHUR? WHERE ARE YOU, SON?

YOU'RE EMBARRASSING ME IN FRONT OF MY FRIENDS, MAN.

COMING UP.. AN ABC WIDE WORLD OF NEWS *SPECIAL REPORT!*

STARRING.. *THE MAN!*

abc news SPECIAL REPORT

WITH CORRESPONDENT ROLAND HEDLEY

MEET JUAN. JUAN IS NINE YEARS OLD AND LIVES IN THE SOUTH BRONX IN NEW YORK CITY.

LIKE OTHER BOYS HIS AGE, JUAN PLAYS STICK BALL AND WORSHIPS REGGIE JACKSON. BUT EVERY MONTH OR SO, WHEN HIS MOTHER'S RENT IS DUE, JUAN DOES SOMETHING MOST OTHER KIDS DO NOT: HE ROBS BANKS.

IT STARTED INNOCUOUSLY ENOUGH WITH HUBCAPS. BUT BY THE TIME JUAN WAS EIGHT, HE HAD BEEN IMPLICATED IN OVER 17 BANK JOBS IN THE METROPOLITAN AREA ALONE..

4 ft.

00430785

GOOD EVENING. I'M ROLAND HEDLEY, AND THIS IS THE STORY OF ONE STREET KID'S INTRODUCTION TO BIG TIME CRIME. IT IS A FAMILIAR STORY, ONE REPEATED WHEREVER POVERTY AND HOPELESSNESS DRIVE CHILDREN TO ACTS OF DESPERATION..

THERE ARE LITERALLY THOUSANDS OF JUANS TODAY, SOME ROBBING BANKS, OTHERS KNOCKING OVER LIQUOR STORES. BUT BECAUSE THEY LEAD SECRET LIVES, THE JUAN YOU SEE HERE IS ACTUALLY A COMPOSITE. THE REAL JUAN DOESN'T REALLY EXIST.

IN FACT, YOUR NAME IS HAROLD, RIGHT, SON?

RIGHT. BUT I KNOW LOTS OF GUYS JUST LIKE JUAN.

GBTrudeau

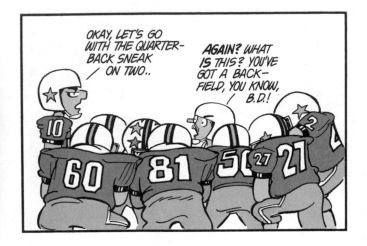

IT WAS GREAT OF YOU TO COME ON DOWN FOR OUR CALL-IN SHOW, PRESIDENT KING!

NOT AT ALL, MARK. I KNOW HOW IMPORTANT IT IS TO KEEP THE CHANNELS OPEN TO STUDENTS! WHAT'S OUR TOPIC?

WELL, I THOUGHT WE MIGHT DISCUSS THE UNIVERSITY MEDAL YOU PRESENTED TODAY.

I THINK STUDENTS WOULD BE FASCINATED TO LEARN HOW AND WHY THE RECIPIENTS OF AWARDS LIKE THIS ARE SELECTED.

TWO SECONDS TO AIR, MARK!

GREAT! I'D BE HAPPY TO..

GOOD EVENING! TONIGHT: "SUCKING UP TO ALUMNI."

MRS. KING? HI, IT'S BETTY.

YES, BETTY..

YOUR HUSBAND ASKED ME TO LET YOU KNOW HE'D BE A LITTLE LATE FOR DINNER TONIGHT.

HE SAID TO TELL YOU HE'D LIKE THREE MARTINIS LINED UP ON THE TABLE IN THE FRONT FOYER.

THAT BAD, HUH?

SO YOU'RE **DENYING** THE COLLEGE HAS DISCRIMINATED AGAINST GAY KITCHEN WORKERS?

LET ME GET BACK TO YOU ON THAT.

GUESS WHAT, JEANIE! MY COUSIN SARAH IS DROPPING OUT OF COLLEGE THIS YEAR TO WORK FOR THE EQUAL RIGHTS AMENDMENT!

NO KIDDING? THE WHOLE YEAR?

UH-HUH. THE ERA EXPIRES NEXT JUNE. IF 38 STATES DON'T RATIFY IT BY THEN, WOMEN WILL LOSE EVERYTHING THEY'VE SPENT THE LAST 15 YEARS FIGHTING FOR!

GEE.. THAT'S INCREDIBLE..

DOES SHE GET OUT OF EXAMS AND EVERYTHING?

YUP. I THINK WE OUGHT TO LOOK INTO IT.

HOWARD, DO YOU THINK I SHOULD TAKE A YEAR OFF FROM SCHOOL TO GO WORK FOR THE ERA?

IT'S OKAY WITH ME. IT'LL IMPROVE THE TEACHER-STUDENT RATIO..

'COURSE, IT'S A COMPLETE WASTE OF TIME, IN CASE YOU HAVEN'T HEARD, ERA IS DEAD.

IT MOST CERTAINLY IS **NOT,** HOWIE!

SURE, IT IS! LOOK, IT WAS A TOUGH BATTLE, BUT IT'S TIME YOU GIRLS FACED FACTS! THE COUNTRY **WANTS** SEX DISCRIMINATION!

THAT DOES IT! FIRST GRADE CAN WAIT!

ADMIT IT, ELLIE, THE BOYS WON FAIR AND SQUARE!

I THINK WE SHOULD DO IT, JEANIE! SOME THINGS ARE JUST MORE IMPORTANT THAN COMPLETING FIRST GRADE ON TIME!

LET'S TELL OUR PARENTS TONIGHT WE'D LIKE TO GO WORK FOR ERA..

HEY, GIRLS!

I JUST THOUGHT OF SOMETHING! WHEN THE ERA DIES, IT'LL PROBABLY BECOME OKAY TO CALL WOMEN "CHICKS" AGAIN! GREAT, HUH?

WOULDN'T HE BE ON SHAKY LEGAL GROUND THERE, ELLIE?

DON'T PRESS YOUR LUCK, HOWARD!

WELL, SEE YOU CHICKS LATER!

MS. LATOUR, ELLIE AND I WOULD LIKE TO ASK YOUR ADVICE ON SOMETHING..

WE'RE THINKING OF DROPPING OUT OF SCHOOL TO WORK FOR PASSAGE OF ERA!

WE REALIZE WE ONLY JUST GOT HERE, BUT TIME'S RUNNING OUT. WE FIGURE WE CAN ALWAYS FINISH THE FIRST GRADE SOME OTHER YEAR.

WELL, GIRLS, I COMMEND YOU FOR YOUR CONCERN, AND I CAN CERTAINLY UNDERSTAND WHY IT MIGHT SEEM IMPORTANT TO YOU TO LEAVE SCHOOL..

UNFORTUNATELY, IT'S AGAINST THE LAW.

IT IS?

UH-OH.. A NEW WRINKLE.

I DON'T KNOW, JEANIE, I MAY HAVE TO DROP OUT OF SCHOOL EVEN IF IT IS ILLEGAL.

I JUST CAN'T SEE STANDING IDLY BY WHILE THE ERA IS IN SUCH TROUBLE.

IT'S NOT ME I'M WORRIED ABOUT. IT MAY BE TOO LATE FOR ME. BUT I'LL BE DARNED IF I'M GOING TO LET MY BABY SISTER GROW UP IN A WORLD OF SEXISM AND INEQUALITY!

SHE'LL THANK ME FOR IT ONE DAY.

HEY, IS THAT A FIST SHE'S MAKING?

THANKS, SISTER!

"..AND WITH THE DISCLOSURE OF RICHARD ALLEN'S LATEST INDISCRETIONS, MANY WHITE HOUSE INSIDERS WONDER WHERE IT WILL ALL END.."

"IN LESS THAN TEN MONTHS, THE PRESIDENT HAS ALREADY BEEN EMBARRASSED BY EVERYONE FROM ALEXANDER HAIG, JAMES WATT AND RAYMOND DONOVAN TO ED MEESE, CASPAR WEINBERGER AND DAVE STOCKMAN."

BOY! THE LINE TO THE WOODSHED SURE IS GETTING LONG..

NEXT!

GOOD MORNING, SIR. LET ME EXPLAIN..

GENTLEMEN, THE TWO OF YOU HAVE DONE NOTHING BUT EMBARRASS ME WITH YOUR SQUABBLING OVER THE NUCLEAR WARNING SHOT..

"BONZO GOES TO WAR" SCENE 82 TAKE 1

I WANT THIS SETTLED ONCE AND FOR ALL! DOES NATO HAVE A DEMONSTRATION BLAST SCENARIO OR NOT? CASPAR?

ABSOLUTELY NOT, SIR. IN FACT, WE MAY NOT EVEN HAVE THE CAPABILITY.

GIVEN THE DELICACY OF THIS KIND OF DEPLOYMENT, THE TECHNICAL ASPECTS ARE VERY WORRISOME. FRANKLY, I'M NOT PERSUADED WE COULD DELIVER SUCH A WEAPON ON TIME AND ON TARGET.

HMM.. WHAT DO YOU THINK, AL?

MR. PRESIDENT, I LIKE TO THINK HIROSHIMA SPEAKS FOR ITSELF.

SO HOW'S THE REACTION BEEN TO OUR NEW PEACE INITIATIVE, ED?

WELL, SIR, I'M AFRAID IT'S STARTING TO BE SEEN AS A LITTLE CYNICAL..

"SALT IN THE WOUND" SCENE TAKE 1

CYNICAL? HOW COME?

BECAUSE WE PROPOSED A PLAN BASED ON MISSILE COUNTS WE KNEW TO BE TOTALLY UNACCEPTABLE TO THE SOVIETS.

AS A RESULT, IT LOOKED LIKE YOU WERE MORE INTERESTED IN SCORING A PUBLIC RELATIONS COUP IN EUROPE THAN IN TAKING ANY REAL STEPS TO REDUCE THE THREAT OF NUCLEAR WAR.

HEY, C'MON, I RENAMED SALT, DIDN'T I?

WELL, YES, SIR, BUT THAT ONLY MEANT YOU WERE COMMITTED TO CHANGING THE STATIONERY.

ED, WHAT ARE YOU GETTING FROM CONGRESS ABOUT STOCKMAN? HAS HIS CREDIBILITY BEEN IRRETRIEVABLY COMPROMISED?

"DEATH OF A SALESMAN" SCENE 81 TAKE 13

WELL, WE SHOULD FIND OUT TODAY. HE WENT UP TO THE HILL TODAY TO PRESENT OUR LATEST BUDGET DEFICIT FIGURES.

GOOD FOR HIM. THAT TAKES GUTS. I'M SURE THE COMMITTEE WILL RESPECT HIM FOR IT.

HA, HA! HA! HA! HA! HA! HA! HA!

NO? OKAY, HOW ABOUT $81 BILLION?

DON'T YOU THINK WE SHOULD GET UP, DEAR? IT'S NEARLY 9:30..

I KNOW.. I'VE JUST BEEN THINKING ABOUT DAVE STOCKMAN..

"CONGRESS MAKES AN OFFER" SCENE 9 TAKE 107

WILL YOU HAVE TO LET HIM GO, DEAR?

NOPE. I'M NOT GIVING IN. AS I TOLD SENATOR BAKER YESTERDAY, CONGRESS CAN LEAN ON ME ALL THEY WANT, BUT DAVID STOCKMAN IS MY.. HEY!

WHAT'S WRONG, DEAR?

WHAT'S.. WHAT'S THAT DOWN AT THE FOOT OF THE BED?..

IT'S.. AIEE!

OH, MY GOD.. THE HEAD OF A TROJAN HORSE!

IT'S TOO BAD YOU'VE BEEN UNDER THE WEATHER, PROFESSOR KISSINGER. YOU'RE MISSING ALL THE HULLABALOO OVER YOUR NEW BOOK!

DON'T WORRY, MR. PERKINS. MY OFFICE KEEPS IN TOUCH.

IT'S A GREAT BOOK, SIR. MOST OF THE CLASS IS WAITING TO BUY IT IN PAPERBACK, BUT I COULDN'T WAIT!

YOU'VE READ IT, ALREADY?

EVERY WORD, SIR! IT'S ENTHRALLING! I'M KIND OF A MEMOIRS BUFF, AND I THINK YOURS IS ONE OF THE BEST I'VE EVER READ!

WHY, THANK YOU, PERKINS, I..

HAVE YOU SEEN EDDIE FISHER'S YET? THAT'S ANOTHER GREAT ONE!

EASY, BARNEY, THEY'RE COMPETITORS.

GET WELL SOON, DOC! ALL YOUR ENEMIES MISS YOU!

SOME PEOPLE JUST WON'T LET OLD WOUNDS HEAL, EH, MR. KISSINGER?

YOU MIGHT SAY THAT.

WELL, I CAN SYMPATHIZE WITH THEIR FEELINGS. WHEN I HELPED CRACK YOUR CHEST LAST MONTH, I MYSELF STARTED THINKING ABOUT MY DAYS IN THE ANTI-WAR MOVEMENT..

IT WAS AN AMAZING MOMENT. AS WE FINISHED UP THE THIRD BYPASS, IT SUDDENLY HIT ME THAT I WAS HOLDING THE HEART OF A MAN WHOSE POLICIES HAD ONCE CONDEMNED THOUSANDS TO DEATH!

THEN I THOUGHT OF MY HIPPOCRATIC OATH AND SEWED YOU UP.

GOOD OATH, THAT.

BECAUSE YOU ASKED FOR IT, CAMPERS, BACK WITH US TODAY IS TOP POP DOC, DAN ASHER, HERE TO PLUG HIS LATEST, "THE MELLOW PARENT: SHARING YOUR SPACE WITH DEPENDENTS." SO WHAT'S THE POOP ON THE BOOK, DANIEL?

WELL, MARK, EVERYONE SEEMS TO BE INTO CHILD-REARING THESE DAYS, SO I JUST FLASHED ON A NEED FOR A NEW PARENTING HOW-TO. IT'S ALL IN THERE—EVERYTHING FROM HIRING YOUR FIRST NANNY TO NONSEXIST CONDITIONING TO WHERE TO HIDE YOUR DOPE!

AND YOU BRING A WEALTH OF EXPERIENCE TO YOUR ADVICE, DON'T YOU, DAN?

I SURE DO. I'VE GOT TWO KIDS FROM MY FIRST MARRIAGE, ONE FROM MY SECOND, AND TWO GREAT STEP-KIDS FROM MY THIRD.

SO THERE'S A LOT OF LAUGHTER AROUND THE ASHER HOUSEHOLD, EH?

ACTUALLY, ONLY ON WEEKENDS. BUT MY LAWYER'S WORKING ON IT.

WE'RE BACK AND RAPPING WITH DR. DAN ASHER, WHO HAS JUST SKYED IN FROM THE COAST TO HYPE HIS LATEST POP EPIC, "THE MELLOW PARENT: SHARING YOUR SPACE WITH DEPENDENTS."

LET'S TAKE IT FROM THE TOP, DOCTOR. WHAT'S YOUR ADVICE TO THE MELLOW MOTHER-TO-BE?

WELL, BASICALLY, IT'S TO GET IN TOUCH WITH YOUR BODY. MORNING SICKNESS, CRAMPS, ACHING BACK—JUST LET IT ALL HAPPEN!

ON THE BIG DAY ITSELF, GO ORGANIC. ANIMALS DON'T USE DRUGS, NEITHER SHOULD YOU. THE BIRTHING PROCESS IS BOTH VIOLENT AND BEAUTIFUL. GET INTO THE PAIN—EXPERIENCE IT FULLY!

AND YOUR ADVICE TO THE MELLOW HUBBY?

TAKE THE DAY OFF. SHOW SOME CLASS.

HI, TED. A LITTLE CHILLY OUT HERE. WHY DON'T YOU COME BACK IN?

NO WAY, RICK. NOT UNTIL SHE AGREES TO LET US DO OUR JOB.

I WON'T WATCH 11 YEARS OF WORK GO DOWN THE DRAIN. THE EPA WAS ONE OF THE FEW AGENCIES IN TOWN WHICH WERE REALLY MAKING A DIFFERENCE!

SEE THOSE CARS DOWN THERE, RICK? WHY, THE AIR'S SO CLEAR NOW YOU CAN READ THEIR LICENSE PLATES FROM HERE!

WOW.. THAT'S AMAZING..

A FEW YEARS AGO, YOU COULDN'T EVEN SEE THE STREET!

OKAY, SIMPSON, YOU WIN. I'LL REINSTATE THE ENFORCEMENT DIVISION.

WILL YOU LET US PROSECUTE POLLUTION VIOLATORS AS WE SEE FIT?

UNTIL SUCH TIME AS THE PRESIDENT CAN GUT THE LAWS, YES.

DO YOU PROMISE?

I PROMISE.

OKAY, I'M COMING IN.

I LIED. YOU'RE FIRED.

AARRGH!

QUICK, SHUT THE WINDOW!

HI, BERNIE! WHAT ARE YOU DOING HERE?

PROFESSOR CAVENDISH IS OUT SICK TODAY. BERNIE'S FILLING IN FOR HIM.

BUT THIS IS INTRO COMPUTER SCIENCE! AREN'T YOU KIND OF SLUMMING, BERNIE?

I DON'T MIND. I'VE PLANNED SOMETHING SPECIAL FOR YOU TODAY—COMPUTER GENERATED WAR GAMES!

WAR GAMES?

I'VE WORKED UP A PROGRAM TO SIMULATE A NUCLEAR CONFRONTATION. EACH OF YOU GETS TO PLAY SOMEONE IN THE COMMAND CHAIN.

I WANT TO BE AL HAIG!

I DIBS BUSH.

ONE AT A TIME, ONE AT A TIME.

CAN I BE THE MAD B-52 PILOT?

GOOD MORNING, ALL, AND WELCOME TO THE WALDEN WAR GAMES. FOR THE NEXT HOUR, WE WILL BE RESPONDING TO COMPUTER SCENARIOS SIMULATING A NUCLEAR CONFRONTATION. THE PROGRAM IS MODELLED AFTER SIMILAR EXERCISES STAGED BY THE PENTAGON.

EACH OF YOU HAS BEEN ASSIGNED A PLACE IN THE CHAIN OF COMMAND. AS THE CRISIS GROWS, YOU MUST USE YOUR CODE BOOKS TO RELAY ORDERS TO YOUR STRATEGIC FORCES.

IN APPROXIMATELY 15 SECONDS, THE PROGRAM WILL APPEAR ON YOUR DISPLAYS. IF AT ANY TIME, YOU WISH TO TRY TO RESOLVE THE CRISIS THROUGH QUIET DIPLOMACY, SIMPLY PRESS THE CLEAR BUTTON.

READY?.. LET THE GAMES BEGIN!

CODE RED! CODE..UH.. NEVER MIND. JUST A FLOCK OF GEESE.

THADIUS! WHAT A NICE SURPRISE! TO WHAT DO WE OWE THE PLEASURE?

DIDN'T DICK TELL YOU? WE'RE GOING BIRDING ON MATAGORDA ISLAND!

WHAT FUN! BUT AREN'T YOU A LITTLE LATE? HAVEN'T ALL THE BIRDS MIGRATED BY NOW?

WELL, A LOT OF THEM HAVE, BUT WE'RE AFRAID IT'S OUR LAST CHANCE!

WATT'S GIVING PARTIAL CONTROL OF THE ISLAND TO THE TEXAS PARKS COMMISSION, WHICH IS SO PRO-DEVELOPMENT IT ONCE VOTED TO TURN A CRITICAL WARBLER HABITAT INTO AN 18-HOLE GOLF COURSE!

OH, DEAR. I BETTER GO GET DICK AT ONCE!

NOT THAT IT WASN'T A PRETTY TOUGH CALL.

HI, DICK. READY TO GO?

I'M AFRAID I HAVE SOME BAD NEWS, THAD. I CAN'T LEAVE. I'VE JUST LEARNED LACEY'S LIFE IS IN DANGER!

WHAT?

NOW, DICK, THAT'S NOTHING TO WORRY ABOUT. I CALLED BILL WEBSTER TODAY AND THE FBI IS CHECKING INTO THE WHOLE MATTER!

I DON'T CARE! SOMEBODY SHOULD BE HERE!

SOMEBODY WILL BE, DEAR. BILL IS SENDING OVER ONE OF HIS BEST YOUNG MEN TO KEEP AN EYE ON ME.

IS HE STOUT? RESOLUTE? WHERE DID HE GO TO SCHOOL?

GO! SCAT! YOU'LL MISS YOUR PLANE!

CERTAINLY IS GOOD TO SEE YOU GENTS BACK IN TEXAS! WHAT TIME WOULD YOU LIKE ME TO RUN YOU OVER TO THE ISLAND?

SOONER THE BETTER, BOB. I'M AFRAID WE'VE MISSED MOST OF THE BIRDS AS IT IS.

WELL, NOT ALL OF 'EM. I SEEN SOME PINTAILS TODAY. THERE'S EVEN SOME WHOOPERS. SINBAD IS STILL HERE, AND MATILDA..

HOW ABOUT IGGY? IS OL' IGGY STILL HERE?

UH..NOPE. I'M AFRAID I GOT SOME BAD NEWS THERE, RICHARD. IGGY HAD A ROUGH WINTER. HE'S..HE'S EXTINCT.

OH..NO! THAT'S TERRIBLE!

YOU MEAN, DEAD, DON'T YOU?

NO, IGGY WAS ONE OF A KIND, THADIUS.

HE WAS THE WHOOPING CRANE'S WHOOPING CRANE.

WE'RE IN LUCK, THAD. MATILDA'S STILL HERE, AND LOOK, THERE'S SAMPSON AND WALTER!

I DON'T KNOW HOW YOU KEEP THEM ALL STRAIGHT, DICK.

WELL, THERE ARE ONLY 73 WHOOPING CRANES ON MATAGORDA, THAD. BESIDES, THEY'RE AS INDIVIDUAL AS YOU AND I. COLOR, MARKINGS, BEHAVIOR PATTERNS, EACH BIRD HAS ITS OWN ECCENTRICITIES.

FOR INSTANCE, SAM THERE IS GAY. AND TILLY WON'T EAT WATER BEETLES UNLESS THEY'VE BEEN STRAINED. AND WALTER SPENDS A LOT OF TIME WITH THE DUCKS.

AND ALL THIS IS CONDONED BY THE WILDLIFE SERVICE?

IT'S A SANCTUARY, THAD.

I THINK I'M BEGINNING TO UNDERSTAND THE WHOOPING CRANE'S BRUSH WITH EXTINCTION.

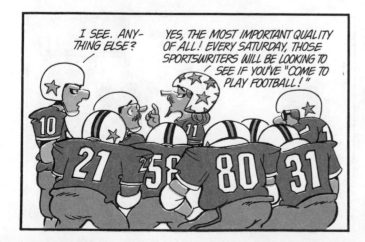

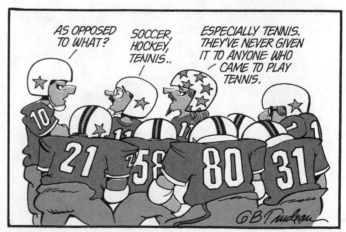

AND NOW IT'S TIME FOR.. "GREAT MOMENTS IN MELLOW"!

AUG. 13, 1975: FIRST CUISINART PROCESSOR CLEARS U.S. CUSTOMS..

WHAT SEASON OF "PROFILES ON PARADE" WOULD BE COMPLETE WITHOUT A VISIT FROM OUR OLD FRIEND, DR. DAN ASHER, TASTEMAKER TO THE MELLOW?

DAN'S LATEST HANDBOOK IS FOR ALL YOU BABY-BOOMERS WHO'VE FINALLY GOTTEN INTO CHILD-REARING, RIGHT, DOCTOR?

THAT'S RIGHT, MARK! I CALL IT, "THE MELLOW PARENT: SHARING YOUR SPACE WITH DEPENDENTS."

WHOA! SOUNDS LIKE ANOTHER TIMELY TITLE, DAN!

FOR SURE, MARK! WITH SO MANY UPSCALE FOLKS GETTING INTO PARENTING THESE DAYS, THERE'S JUST A BIG NEED FOR YOUR BASIC HOW-TO!

IN "THE MELLOW PARENT," I DISCUSS SUCH PROBLEMS AS LOOKING FOR A GOOD HOUSE-KEEPER, PREVENTING YOUR BABY FROM EATING YOUR FERNS, AND THE IMPORTANCE OF BUDGETING QUALITY TIME.

WHAT'S "QUALITY TIME," DAN?

THAT'S A SMALL PART OF THE DAY YOU SET ASIDE TO SPEND WITH YOUR KID. IT DOESN'T HAVE TO BE MUCH, TEN MINUTES IS USUALLY ENOUGH, BUT IT HAS TO BE QUALITY! YOU CAN'T JUST WATCH T.V. —YOU HAVE TO FOCUS ON THE CHILD'S NEEDS.

WHAT IF ONE OF ITS NEEDS IS MORE TIME?

THAT'S QUANTITY TIME. I'M NOT REALLY TALK-ING ABOUT THE PROB-LEM CHILD HERE, MARK.

G B Trudeau

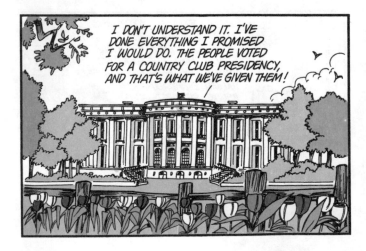

..AND, OF COURSE, HE'S GOT ANOTHER AUGUST VACATION COMING UP, WHICH THE PRESIDENT PROBABLY WON'T EVEN ENJOY BECAUSE HE'LL BE WORKING SO HARD.

OH? DOING WHAT?

MAKING TOUGH DECISIONS THAT ONLY HE, AS PRESIDENT, CAN MAKE.

I SEE. ANY OTHER BIG WORKING VACATIONS ON THE DRAWING BOARD?

WELL, IT'S SUPPOSED TO BE A SECRET, BUT HE'S THINKING OF TAKING NEXT YEAR OFF.

THE WHOLE YEAR?

THAT'S RIGHT. OF COURSE, HE'D BE IN CONSTANT TOUCH WITH THE WHITE HOUSE.

EV, LET'S TAKE THE GLOVES OFF, OKAY? GIVEN THE CURRENT HARD TIMES, DO YOU THINK REAGAN'S RELENTLESS VACATION SCHEDULE IS WINNING HIM ANY POINTS IN THE SENSITIVITY DEPARTMENT?

AS A MATTER OF FACT, MARK, I DO. YOU SEE, THE PRESIDENT GREW UP DURING THE DEPRESSION. HE REMEMBERS THE OLD HIGH SOCIETY MOVIES AND WHAT A GREAT ESCAPE THEY WERE FOR POOR PEOPLE..

THAT'S WHY HE TAKES OFF SO MUCH TIME. IT'S JUST MR. REAGAN'S WAY OF GETTING PEOPLE'S MINDS OFF THEIR PROBLEMS. THANKS TO TELEVISION, WHEN HE TAKES A VACATION, THE WHOLE COUNTRY GETS TO GO ALONG!

SOUNDS GREAT! WHERE ARE WE OFF TO NEXT?

BEVERLY HILLS! PALM SPRINGS! NEW YORK! YOU TELL US! THEY'RE YOUR VACATIONS, AMERICA!

EV, LET'S TALK FOR A MINUTE ABOUT ONE OF THE PRESIDENT'S MOST MEMORABLE VACATIONS—LAST SPRING'S DISASTROUS TRIP TO BARBADOS.

AS YOU KNOW, THOSE FEW DAYS OF R&R COST THE TAXPAYERS MILLIONS OF DOLLARS, AS WELL AS THE GOOD WILL OF SEVERAL CARIBBEAN LEADERS CYNICALLY ADDED TO THE SCHEDULE AS AN AFTERTHOUGHT..

MOREOVER, IT EXHAUSTED THE PRESIDENT, MAKING THE TRIP POINTLESS. ANY COMMENT?

HE ALSO RUINED HIS FILM AND GOT A SUNBURN. HEY, HAVEN'T YOU EVER HAD A VACATION WHERE EVERYTHING WENT WRONG?

PLAIN BAD LUCK, HUH?

LOOK, THE GUY'S HUMAN. HE EVEN LOST HIS TRAVELER'S CHECKS!

YEAH, LET ME SPEAK TO REAGAN'S VACATION MAN!

YOU GOT HIM, GUY!

LISTEN, MAN, WHAT I WANT TO KNOW IS WHY THE PRESIDENT'S TAKING ALL THESE VACATIONS WHEN 9% OF THE WORK FORCE IS ON PERMANENT VACATION, DIG? ANSWER ME THAT, MR. VACATION COORDINATOR!

I MEAN, I'VE BEEN OUT OF WORK SINCE APRIL, AND..

HEY, HEY, LIGHTEN UP, GUY! YOU MAY NOT BE WORKING RIGHT NOW, BUT LET ME ASK YOU THIS: HOW'S YOUR TAN? HUH?

I'M BLACK.

EXACTLY! SO THE SUMMER WASN'T A TOTAL LOSS, RIGHT?

HEY, MIKE, YOU SEEN BOOPSIE?

YEAH. SHE WENT DOWN TO THE OPENING OF THE NEW JANE FONDA FITNESS CENTER.

WHAT?

DIDN'T SHE TELL YOU? SHE SIGNED UP FOR SOME SESSIONS.

I DON'T BELIEVE THAT CHICK..

SHE WAS PRETTY EXCITED. JANE FONDA IS HERE TO LEAD THE FIRST WEEK OF WORKOUTS HERSELF!

BRAN! NUTS! GERM! SEED! WE DON'T WANT YOUR CORPORATE GREED!

>PUFF! PUFF!< AM I DOING IT RIGHT, MISS FONDA?

A LITTLE LOWER.. LOWER.. WHAT ARE YOU FEELING?

I FEEL A BURN.. >PUFF!<.. BUT IT'S A GOOD BURN!

WHAT ELSE DO YOU FEEL?

I FEEL.. A SURGE OF PRIDE, OF SELF-ESTEEM.. I FEEL I'VE BEEN RIPPED OFF BY A FALSE FEMALE IDEAL!

WHAT ELSE? LISTEN TO YOUR BODY!

I FEEL.. SENSITIVE! NO, SENSITIZED! I FEEL POLITICALLY SENSITIZED!

GOOD! NOW THE OTHER SIDE!

WOW..THAT WAS SOME WORKOUT, MISS FONDA..

WELL, I'M JUST TRYING TO KEEP WOMEN LIKE YOURSELVES FROM MAKING THE MISTAKES I DID..

IT TOOK ME 20 YEARS OF SELF-ABUSE, OF DIET GUM AND BINGEING AND VOMITING AND DEXEDRINE AND DIURETICS, BEFORE I LEARNED THE SECRET TO LOSING WEIGHT: EAT LESS AND EXERCISE MORE!

WOW..

GEE..

WHAT A BREAKTHROUGH.

HOW COME IT TOOK 20 YEARS?

MALE DOCTORS HID THE TRUTH FROM ME.

THERE YOU ARE! DO YOU KNOW WHAT TIME IT IS?

SORRY, B.D., BUT A GOOD WORKOUT TAKES TIME!

GOD, WILL YOU LOOK AT YOU! YOU'RE A MESS! SWEATING ALL OVER THE CARPET LIKE SOME..

I MADE A BREAKTHROUGH TODAY, B.D...

ABOUT 40 MINUTES INTO THE WORKOUT, I BEGAN TO FEEL REALLY GOOD ABOUT MYSELF! A FEW MINUTES LATER, IT SUDDENLY HIT ME THAT I'D SPENT MY WHOLE LIFE INTERNALIZING SOME DUMB FEMININE IDEAL!

GREAT.

MISS FONDA WAS AMAZED! I'M ONLY UP TO BEGINNER'S BUTTOCKS!

IT'S TRUE, B.D.! GETTING IN SHAPE AND POLITICAL ACTIVISM ARE RELATED!

WHAT GARBAGE! WERE THE SPARTANS POLITICALLY ACTIVE? ARE THE CINCINNATI BENGALS?

IF YOU LOOK AT YOUR HISTORY, ALL THE PEOPLE WHO PROMOTED PHYSICAL FITNESS THROUGH THE AGES HAVE BEEN CONSERVATIVE. BELIEVE ME, LIBERALS KNOW NOTHING ABOUT GETTING IN SHAPE, ESPECIALLY LADY LIBERALS!

OH, YEAH?

YEAH!

WHAT ABOUT THE BIKINI SCENE IN "GOLDEN POND"?

THAT WAS ALL SPECIAL EFFECTS! JEEZ, BOOPSIE, SOMETIMES YOU CAN BE SO GULLIBLE!

MISS FONDA, MY BOYFRIEND HAS BEEN GIVING ME A LOT OF GRIEF ABOUT YOUR PROGRAM. HE SAYS IT'S ONLY FOR THE TRENDY MIDDLE CLASS.

WELL, THAT MAY HAVE BEEN A PROBLEM IN THE PAST..

BUT STARTING THIS FALL, MY BEVERLY HILLS WORKOUT SALON WILL BE SETTING UP FITNESS OUT-REACH CLINICS TO HELP MIGRANT FARM WORKERS MEET THEIR EXERCISE NEEDS!

MIGRANT FARM WORKERS?

RIGHT.

DON'T THEY ALREADY GET ENOUGH EXERCISE?

ONLY IN THEIR UPPER ARMS. THEY COMPLETELY NEGLECT THOSE IMPORTANT ABDOMINALS.

HEY.. IS THAT A KNITTED BROW I SEE?

WHAT?

YOU'RE WORRYING ABOUT SOMETHING. WHICH IS FUNNY, BECAUSE I AM, TOO. WHAT ARE YOU WORRYING ABOUT?

OH.. NOTHING.

OH, YES, YOU ARE. I'LL BET IT'S THE SAME THING I'M WORRYING ABOUT. C'MON, TELL ME.

AMNIOCENTESIS.

OH.. NO, THAT'S NOT IT. I WAS WORRYING ABOUT THE CLUTCH ON THE VOLVO.

AMNIOCENTESIS? YOU'RE WORRIED ABOUT AMNIOCENTESIS?

OF COURSE, I'M WORRIED ABOUT IT. TOMORROW I HAVE TO GO IN FOR AN ABSOLUTELY DREADFUL PROCEDURE, FOLLOWING WHICH I STAND A 1-IN-50 CHANCE OF RECEIVING TERRIBLE NEWS.

MEANWHILE, I'M TURNING INTO THIS MISSHAPEN BLIMPO WITH PERSISTENT NAUSEA, PREMATURE BACKACHE, VIOLENT MOOD SWINGS..

HMM.. SOUNDS LIKE YOU COULD USE SOME CHEERING UP!

..AND A HUSBAND WHO KEEPS TRYING TO CHEER ME UP.

HEY, GIVE ME A CHANCE.. I'VE GOT SOME NEW HAND SHADOWS.

WELL, THAT'S IT, JOANIE. ALL DONE!

EVERYTHING WENT FINE. I SHOULD HAVE THE RESULTS FOR YOU IN A COUPLE OF WEEKS.

HOW'RE YOU HOLDING UP? THAT WASN'T REALLY SO BAD, WAS IT?

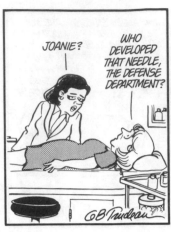
JOANIE?

WHO DEVELOPED THAT NEEDLE, THE DEFENSE DEPARTMENT?

WELL, IT'S ALL OVER, BABE. NOW YOU CAN STOP WORRYING.

I'M AFRAID I WON'T STOP WORRYING UNTIL THE RESULTS ARE IN. AND EVEN IF I CHECK OUT, THEN I HAVE TO START WORRYING ABOUT PRE-NATAL CARE AND EXERCISE AND DIET AND NUTRITION..

..AND.. AIIEE!

WHAT? WHAT'S WRONG?

I ALMOST DRANK SOME WINE..

JOANIE, ARE YOU SURE YOU'VE DONE THIS BEFORE?

BOY, I WISH I COULD SHAKE THIS FUNK. TODAY I GOT SO DE-PRESSED I CAME HOME FROM WORK AFTER LUNCH.

GOOD THING YOU'RE NOT PRESIDENT, HUH?

DON'T GIVE ME THAT OLD LINE, RICK. IF I WERE PRESIDENT RIGHT NOW, I WOULDN'T GET PREGNANT!

WHAT IF YOU WERE NEARING MENOPAUSE WHILE IN OFFICE, AND YOU STILL WANTED ONE MORE KID?

WELL, IN THAT CASE, I'D..UH..

I'D JUST GO HAVE IT AT CAMP DAVID. I WOULDN'T START ANY WARS OR ANYTHING.

OH, SURE, AND WHAT ABOUT DO-MESTICALLY? WHAT HAPPENS TO THE POOR FOR NINE MONTHS?

WELL, I'VE GOT SOME GOOD NEWS FOR YOU FOLKS.

YOU DO?

YUP. THE FETUS CHECKED OUT OKAY. THERE'S NO EVIDENCE OF ANY ABNORMAL-ITIES.

WELL, THAT'S A RELIEF!

BY THE WAY, SINCE YOU SAID YOU WANTED TO KNOW, IT'S A BOY. AND HE SHOULD HAVE SANDY HAIR, FRECKLES, AND AN APTITUDE FOR MATH.

BOY, THEY'VE REALLY PERFECTED THAT TEST, HAVEN'T THEY?

HE'LL ALSO BE A RED SOX FAN.

PLEASED TO MEET YOU, MR. CHAIRMAN. I'M ROLAND BURTON HEDLEY, JR.

ROLAND HERE IS WITH ABC NEWS, ARAFAT, ONE OF THE AMERICAN NETWORKS.

AH, YES. A PLEASURE, MR. HEDLEY. WE ARE MOST GRATEFUL TO NETWORK TELEVISION FOR SHOWING AMERICANS THE REAL ISRAEL!

JUST CALLING IT THE WAY WE SEE IT, SIR.

OF COURSE, YOU ARE, MR. HEDLEY.

SO WHAT HAVE YOU BEEN UP TO, MR. CHAIRMAN? OUT POSING WITH BABIES AGAIN?

THEY'RE GETTING HARDER TO FIND. I HAD TO KISS A CHRISTIAN KID THIS MORNING.

WHOA! YOU MEAN, YOU'RE EVEN RUNNING OUT OF INNOCENT CIVILIANS?

YOU WANT TO KNOW WHAT KIND OF PEOPLE THESE ISRAELIS ARE? THE TWO DAYS AFTER I DISCUSSED ENDORSING U.N. RESOLUTIONS 242 AND 338, THEY BOMBED BEIRUT AT EXACTLY 2:42 P.M. AND 3:38 P.M.!

CUTE TOUCH.

FOR THE ISRAELIS, IT IS GAMES. FOR US, OUR EXISTENCE AS A PEOPLE IS AT STAKE.

WANT TO TALK IT OUT, MR. CHAIRMAN?

NO, NO, I CAN SEE THAT YOU'RE BUSY. YOU'RE PREOCCUPIED WITH GETTING AT THE TRUTH ABOUT THIS UNCONSCIONABLE INVASION.

PRESS CONFERENCE!

YOU JOURNALISTS. YOU'RE INSATIABLE!

BELIEVE ME, GENTLEMEN, WHETHER WE LIVE OR DIE IS IMMATERIAL. WHAT THE ISRAELI INVASION HAS DONE IS EXPOSE THE INJUSTICE OF THE PALESTINIAN PLIGHT!

SO YOU THINK THAT ISRAEL HAS DAMAGED ITSELF MORE THAN THE P.L.O., MR. CHAIRMAN?

OF COURSE. WHAT AMAZES ME IS THAT IN TWO SHORT MONTHS OF WANTON BRUTALITY, THE ISRAELIS HAVE SQUANDERED 30 YEARS OF MORAL CAPITAL!

THIS IS NOT THE ISRAEL I KNEW.

HEY, YASSER, GIVE US A BREAK.

I ASK YOU, GENTLEMEN, DO I LOOK LIKE A MONSTER? IS YASSER ARAFAT THE VICIOUS TERRORIST ISRAEL WOULD HAVE YOU BELIEVE?

IT IS TIME THE WORLD SAW THE PALESTINIANS AS PEOPLE, AS VICTIMS OF A TERRIBLE INJUSTICE!

CHAIRMAN ARAFAT, I WONDER IF I MIGHT JUST FOLLOW UP ON THE MATTER OF YOUR PERSONAL APPEARANCE..

A LOT OF AMERICANS WOULD LOVE TO KNOW HOW YOU GET YOUR BEARD TO LOOK LIKE YOU'VE ALWAYS GOT A 3-DAY GROWTH.

ANY OTHER QUESTIONS?

SERIOUSLY, DO YOU TRIM IT JUST BEFORE YOU GO TO BED OR WHAT?

..AND WE FEEL WE'VE BEEN MORE THAN FLEXIBLE DURING THE NEGOTIATIONS. THE DROPPING OF OUR DEMAND FOR A LIST OF P.L.O. EVACUEES IS A GOOD EXAMPLE.

BUT WHY DID YOU NEED SUCH A LIST IN THE FIRST PLACE?

TO MONITOR COMPLIANCE, OF COURSE. TO MAKE SURE ALL THE TERRORISTS LEFT.

BUT ONCE YOU HAD ALL THEIR NAMES AND ADDRESSES IN YOUR COMPUTER, COULDN'T THAT HAVE LED TO ALL KINDS OF ABUSE?

ABUSE? LIKE WHAT?

WELL, LIKE, WHAT WOULD'VE KEPT YOU FROM SENDING THE GUERRILLAS A LOT OF JUNK MAIL?

WE WERE PREPARED TO OFFER CERTAIN GUARANTEES.

I'M JUST DELIGHTED YOUR YOUNG MAN DOESN'T MIND MY BORROWING YOU FOR A FEW WEEKS, DEAR. IT'S SO DREARY CAMPAIGNING BY ONESELF.

I'M PLEASED, TOO, LACEY. IT'S NICE TO GET OUT OF WASHINGTON FOR A WHILE.

I'LL WANT YOU TO STAY AT OUR HOUSE, OF COURSE, AND YOU CAN USE THE LIBRARY AS YOUR OFFICE.

BASICALLY, YOUR RESPONSIBILITIES WILL BE TO SCHEDULE A FEW APPEARANCES AND ARRANGE A SMALL MEDIA CAMPAIGN. THAT'S ABOUT ALL YOU'D REALLY HAVE TO DO.

WHAT ABOUT RECRUITING CANVASSERS?

HMM..TOO LATE FOR THAT. WE MIGHT HAVE TO USE THE SERVANTS AGAIN.

HI. IT'S THE PREGNANT LADY.

HI, PREGNANT LADY. HOW'S IT GOING OUT THERE?

PRETTY GOOD. I'M ALL SETTLED INTO MY NEW OFFICE, AND LACEY IS ALREADY OUT CAMPAIGNING.

I MUST SAY, IT'S REALLY AN EXPERIENCE WATCHING HER MEET WITH PEOPLE. SHE'S CERTAINLY NOT SHY ABOUT STANDING ON HER RECORD!

..AND HERE ARE SOME OF THE VOTES I'M PROUDEST OF.

HMM.. NOT BAD.

BOY! LOOKS LIKE YOU VOTED YOUR CONSCIENCE RIGHT DOWN THE LINE!

ANOTHER INVITE JUST CAME IN, BOSS. THE BAY AREA GAY ALLIANCE WOULD LIKE YOU TO SPEAK TO THEM TOMORROW.

THE GAY ALLIANCE?

ACTUALLY, YOU MIGHT WANT TO DO THAT ONE. I'VE BEEN LOOKING OVER THE LATEST DEMOGRAPHICS, AND YOUR DISTRICT IS NOW HEAVILY GAY.

GOODNESS! IT IS?

THAT'S RIGHT.

MY, HOW THINGS CHANGE! YES, BY ALL MEANS LET'S GO. I'D LOVE TO HEAR WHAT THEY HAVE TO SAY!

THAT'S VERY OPEN OF YOU, BOSS.

NOT AT ALL. I'VE ALWAYS FOUND CONFIRMED BACHELORS JUST SO FASCINATING!

I'D LIKE TO THANK THE GAY ALLIANCE FOR INVITING ME HERE TONIGHT. CHATTING WITH ALL OF YOU HAS BEEN MOST INSTRUCTIVE.

ALSO, I MUST SAY, IT'S REFRESHING TO MEET A GROUP OF CONSTITUENTS WITH SUCH FINE MANNERS. I'M ALSO VERY IMPRESSED WITH HOW NICELY YOU ALL DRESS.

THE ONLY THING I MIGHT QUIBBLE WITH IS YOUR HAIR. SOME OF YOU BOYS HAVE TERRIBLY SHORT HAIRCUTS. HAIR THAT SHORT LOOKS FINE ON NAVY CADETS, BUT OTHERWISE IT MAKES YOU LOOK AWFULLY YOUNG.

UH.. LACEY..

NEVER MIND. MINOR POINT. THANKS AGAIN.

IT'S NO USE. ACCORDING TO MY CALCULATIONS, THERE'S JUST NO WAY OUT OF IT THIS TIME!

OUT OF WHAT, ZONK?

GRADUATION. THE ONLY THING BETWEEN ME AND THE REAL WORLD IS ONE UNFLUNKABLE CERAMICS COURSE!

GOOD. THEN YOU CAN COME IN WITH ME TODAY AND SIGN UP FOR SOME JOB INTERVIEWS.

JOB INTERVIEWS?

UH-HUH.

LET ME RECHECK MY FIGURES.

MAYBE YOU CAN BREAK THE KILN.

JOB INTERVIEWS? YOU'RE ACTUALLY SIGNING UP FOR JOB INTERVIEWS?

WE'RE SENIORS, ZONK. WHAT OTHER CHOICE DO WE HAVE?

BUT I DON'T KNOW THE FIRST THING ABOUT JOB INTERVIEWS! I'D BE EATEN ALIVE!

NO, YOU WOULDN'T, ZONK..

IT'S REALLY NO BIG DEAL. YOU JUST TALK TO THE RECRUITER FOR TWENTY MINUTES OR SO. ALL YOU HAVE TO DO IS BE YOURSELF.

BUT.. BUT WHAT IF THEY OFFER ME A JOB?

WELL, YOU ALWAYS RUN THAT RISK.

NAME?

HARRIS, ZONKER.

WHICH COMPANIES ARE YOU INTERESTED IN INTERVIEWING WITH?

DEPENDS. WHAT HAVE YOU GOT?

MR. HARRIS, THERE ARE OVER 200 COMPANIES RECRUITING ON CAMPUS. WHAT ARE YOUR GENERAL AREAS OF INTEREST?

AERODYNAMICS. DESIGNER JEANS. ROOFING SUPPLIES. THAT SORT OF THING.

WHAT SORT OF THING?

YOU KNOW, LIQUIDITY. POINT-OF-SALE. MARGIN ACCOUNTS. FAST LANE.

CAREFUL, ZONK. YOU'LL PEAK BEFORE THE INTERVIEWS.

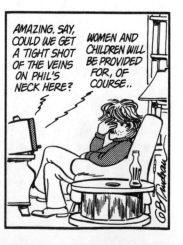

FRIENDS, AS YOU KNOW, THE LAST 20 MONTHS HAVE BEEN A TERRIBLE ORDEAL FOR ME. BUT I THINK IT'S NOW TIME TO LET BYGONES BE BYGONES, EVEN THOUGH IT MEANS PUTTING DOZENS OF PERJURERS BACK ON THE STREETS.

IN THAT SPIRIT, I'VE ALSO DECIDED TO CALL OFF MY FORMER COMPANY'S INVESTIGATION OF THE SENATORS INVESTIGATING ME. I'M GIVING ORRIN HATCH AND THE REST OF THE COMMITTEE A CLEAN BILL OF HEALTH!

NOW **THAT'S** CLASS!

WHAT A GUY!

ALSO, TO THANK ALL THE ELECTED OFFICIALS HERE TONIGHT, I PROMISE TO ENDORSE **EACH** OF YOU FOR RE-ELECTION!

NO! **NO!** THAT'S OKAY!

WOULDN'T HEAR OF IT RAY!

THANKS ANYWAY!

SIGH..

HI, SAILOR! WELCOME TO THE NEIGHBORHOOD. THE NAME'S ALICE P. SCHWARTZMAN! WHO ARE YOU?

UH..DUKE. THE NAME'S DUKE.

PLEASED TO MEET YOU, DUCK. WANT PART OF MY PAPER? IT'S ONLY THREE WEEKS OLD!

YEAH.. YOU GOT THE SPORTS SECTION?

SURE. YOU FOLLOW THE PONIES?

NAH. I JUST PUT MY LAST TEN BUCKS ON THE BREWERS.

THIS AIN'T YOUR DAY, DUCKS.

HEY, WHO'S THIS JOHN DE LOREAN GUY WHO'S ALL OVER THE PAPERS?

HE'S A BIG CAR EXECUTIVE WHO GOT BUSTED FOR TRYING TO BUY A TON OF COCAINE.

OH..

HOW A SMART, GOOD-LOOKING FELLAH LIKE THAT COULD GET IN SO MUCH TROUBLE IS BEYOND ME!

WHAT A LIFE HE HAD, DUCKS! A GOLDEN BOY AT G.M., THREE GORGEOUS WIVES, THEN HIS OWN CAR COMPANY! SOMEBODY OUGHT TO MAKE A MOVIE OF HIS STORY. IT'D MAKE **MILLIONS!**

HELLO?

OF COURSE, THAT PERSON WOULD HAVE TO KNOW SOMETHING ABOUT THE DRUG WORLD.

A **MOVIE!** THAT'S A HELLUVA IDEA, LADY! "THE JOHN DE LOREAN STORY" IS A **NATURAL!**

TOO BAD YOU DON'T HAVE THE RIGHTS, DUCKY.

I CAN GET 'EM! I'LL CALL HIS LAWYER. I **KNOW** THIS WORLD — FAST CARS, CHEAP DRUGS, CHEAP CARS, AND FAST WOMEN — THIS IS MY /SCENE!

GOOD LORD, I EVEN KNOW SOME OF THE PRINCIPALS! HETRICK AND ARRINGTON, THE TWO GUYS BUSTED WITH DE LOREAN! WE USED TO DOCK AT THE SAME WHARF IN FT. LAUDERDALE!

HELL, I EVEN ONCE LOANED THEM MY DECK GUN!

OKAY, I'M IN! HERE'S A DIME FOR THE CALL!

"COMING UP: THE MELLOW BULLETIN BOARD.."

"..BUT FIRST THE RESULTS OF THE BLOOMINGDALE'S/CALVIN KLEIN PRO-AM 20 KM. TEN-SPEED PERRIER CLASSIC.."

FEW GUESTS OF WBBY INSPIRE MORE AWE IN OUR LISTENING AUDIENCE THAN DR. DAN ASHER, AUTHOR OF "THE MELLOW PARENT." TONIGHT HE'S BACK WITH US TO DISCUSS HIS CHAPTER ON EDUCATION..

DOCTOR, A LOT OF UPSCALE PARENTS ARE TORN ON THE SUBJECT OF WHETHER TO SEND THEIR KIDS TO A PRIVATE OR A PUBLIC SCHOOL. WHERE DO YOU COME DOWN ON THIS TRICKY QUESTION?

WELL, BASICALLY, MARK, I'M VERY PRO-PREP.

SOME MELLOW PARENTS WILL TRY TO TELL YOU THAT THEY DON'T WANT THEIR CHILDREN TO GROW UP WITH JUST OTHER PRIVILEGED KIDS, THAT THEY WANT THEM TO HAVE FRIENDS FROM ALL WALKS OF LIFE..

NOTHING COULD BE MORE ABSURD. AS PRESIDENT REAGAN HIMSELF HAS SO DRAMATICALLY DEMONSTRATED, THERE'S NO POINT IN GROWING UP WITH THE GREAT UNWASHED IF YOU HAVE NO INTENTION OF EVER ASSOCIATING WITH THEM AGAIN!

MOST PREPPIES WILL NEVER HAVE TO INTER-ACT WITH THE DISADVANTAGED, EXCEPT THOSE IN SERVICE POSITIONS, SO WHY FORCE THEM TO RUB SHOULDERS DURING THEIR CHILDHOODS? BASICALLY, IT'S TERRIBLY IRRELEVANT!

BEING EXPOSED TO THE POOR IS IRRELEVANT?

RIGHT. IT'S LIKE HAVING TO TAKE LATIN.

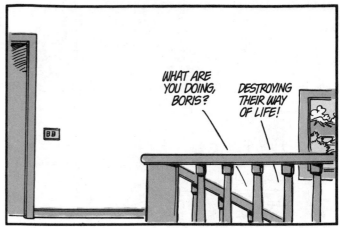

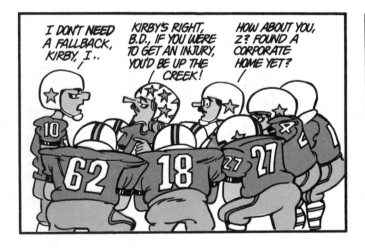

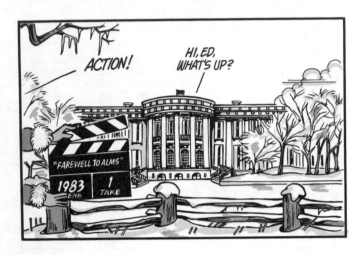

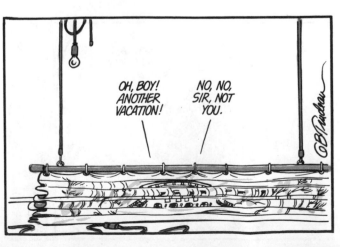